New York State
Probate Records

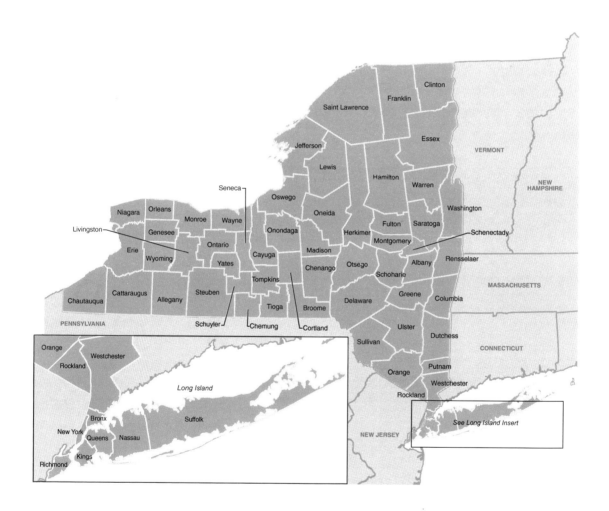

New York State Probate Records

A Genealogist's Guide to Testate and Intestate Records

Second Edition

Gordon L. Remington, FUGA, FASG

New England Historic
Genealogical Society
2011

ISBN-13: 978-0-88082-243-5

Library of Congress Control Number: 2010942269

Cover design by Ann Conneman. Cover photo © Eric Noyen/123RF.
Maps by Mapping Specialists, Inc., Fitchburg, Wisconsin
Printed by Yurchak Printing, Landisville, Pennsylvania

NEW ENGLAND HISTORIC GENEALOGICAL SOCIETY®
99–101 Newbury Street
Boston, Massachusetts 02116-3007
www.AmericanAncestors.org

Contents

Preface and Acknowledgments

New York State Probate Records: A Genealogist's Guide to Testate and Intestate Records is a tool to help you locate probate records that have been recorded in New York State over the last three centuries. To the genealogical purist, the title "Probate Records" may not be quite accurate, for technically this term refers only to persons leaving wills (testate) and not to those who died without one (intestate). Wills must be "proved" (probated) as to their authenticity before an executor can be appointed, whereas the issuance of letters of administration requires only a statement that the decedent left an estate but no will.

The word probate, however, has come to mean the general class of records associated with an estate. Even *Black's Law Dictionary* (6th edition) states that "in current usage this term has been expanded to refer to the legal process wherein the estate of a decedent is administered." In New York today, the court in charge of probating estates is the Surrogate's Court—a state court represented in New York's sixty-two counties by a "surrogate." This book could have been called *New York Surrogate's Records*, but it covers many more records than those in the local surrogate's courts.

There are a number of "guides" to New York probate records, notably Harry Macy Jr.'s two-part article on New York probate records before and after 1787 in *The NYG&B Newsletter* and the New York State Archives Information Leaflet #3—Probate Records. These guides are very informative as to the history, nature, and current location of New York probate records of interest to the genealogist, but they deal mainly with records from the colonial period and nineteenth century. Moreover, they are limited in terms of specific information guiding you to the records you need.

New York State Probate Records seeks to do just that—not only to describe the records, but also to give information on how to access them. Unless you live in Albany or New York City, you are most likely to consult New York probate records on microfilm at the Family History Library in Salt Lake City or through its network of worldwide Family History Centers. The Family History Library has the best collection of New York records outside of New York State. *New York State Probate Records* saves you the time of correlating the Family History Library Catalog to the records in the New York State Archives and local surrogate's courts by giving you the information necessary to order microfilm to your nearest Family History Center.

But *New York State Probate Records* goes beyond providing access to the collections of the Family History Library. Current (Fall 2010) contact information is given for each of New York's sixty-two county surrogate's courts as well as for other repositories in which original probate records are located.

In addition, references to published abstracts in both books and periodicals are given. Published abstracts in particular are useful when they contain every-name indexes—often revealing "hidden" relationships not evident in an index to the name of the decedent only.

There are two caveats in using *New York State Probate Records*. The first should be obvious. No matter how current a guide of this nature is when it goes to press, address and phone numbers are bound to change. Needless to say, Internet and email addresses can change almost as soon as they are published.

Moreover, advances in technology are changing access to New York State probate records as this book goes to press. Each of New York State's surrogate's courts is currently or soon will be digitizing their pre-1970 records (post-1970 records are already digitized) and providing access to the digitized records at the courthouse. Some county surrogate's courts have made their records available on the Internet—or at least the indexes necessary to find them. As the digitization is in process and not yet complete, it was not practical to give the current status for each county. Contact with the surrogate's court in the county of interest should be made to learn the progress of digitization in that county.

The availability of probate records on the Internet, however, does not obviate the need to consult the original records (at the court house and/or on microfilm) and published abstracts thereof. As stated earlier, *New York State Probate Records* provides the information necessary to access probate records in these formats.

The second caveat is less obvious unless explicitly stated. *New York State Probate Records* presumes that as a genealogist you are already familiar with the probate process and basic terminology associated with probate records. This is primarily a guide to finding the records, not a description of the probate process. There is some discussion of processes when necessary to understand records. Especially noteworthy is a detailed discussion of the post-1829 petition to probate or administer an estate that named all the heirs-at-law of a decedent. Though not exclusive to New York State, the petition was instituted there much earlier than the rest of the country and provides a great source for overcoming New York's lack of nineteenth-century vital records. If you find you need additional information, however, there are numerous books—such as Val Greenwood's *Researcher's Guide to American Genealogy* and Ancestry's *The Source*—to provide you with the necessary terminology and definitions to understand the records.

Acknowledgments

Putting together a work of this nature could not have been accomplished without a great deal of help. I gratefully acknowledge, therefore, those who assisted me in this effort.

The first edition of *New York State Probate Records* was prepared with help from John W. Remington, DeeDee Remington, Lyudmila Bagdasarova, Linda Turner, A.G.®, Darrell Hooker, A.G.®, Laura DeGrazia, C.G.®, Edward H. L. Smith III, Harry Macy, Jr., FASG, Coreen Hallenbeck, and David Paul Davenport, PhD.

Roger D. Joslyn, FASG, and Leslie Corn, MA, assisted with New York City advice in both editions.

For this second edition, Roger Joslyn also assisted with information on surrogate's records in Hudson Valley counties. Dawne Slater-Putt and John Beatty of the Allen County Public Library in Fort Wayne, Indiana, assisted with citations to periodicals from PERSI. William Ruddock also contributed to the second edition with insights on the current status of surrogates records in some counties. I am also grateful for the contributions of James D. Folts, Head of Reference Services at the New York State Archives.

This second edition could not have been completed without the help of the staff and volunteers of the New England Historic Genealogical Society. In particular Michael J. Leclerc, director of special projects; Carolyn Sheppard Oakley, creative director; Scott C. Steward, director of publications; Penelope Stratton, managing editor; Henry B. Hoff, editor of the *Register*; and volunteer Meredith Gabrilska. Ann Conneman designed the handsome cover, and Ginevra Morse prepared the index.

I would also like to thank those in my family who came before and who fostered my interest in genealogy: my parents John Leighton and Betty Mae (Thomas) Remington and my brother Douglas Bradford Remington, to whom I dedicate this work.

Without the help of all of you, this work would not have been possible.

Thank you,

Gordon L. Remington, FUGA, FASG
Salt Lake City, Utah
October 2010

Using this Book

New York State Probate Records: A Guide to Genealogist's Guide to Testate and Intestate Records is designed to give you the tools you need to conduct research in probate records in New York. Whether you are tracing your family in the Dutch colonial era or modern New York State, you will find what you need in these pages.

While working with original documents is optimal, accessing probate records in New York State does not always require a personal visit to the county surrogate's office. Records are available in a wide variety of easily-accessible formats, including abstracts, transcriptions, and imaged copies (digital and/or microfilm) of original records. You will find all the tools you need to locate these various formats here.

The book is divided into three sections: Understanding Probate Records, Surrogate's Courts, and Appendixes.

Understanding Probate Records

The first section of this book provides a history of the probate process in what is today the state of New York. Starting with the Dutch settlement, through the English colonial era, and into the modern period, you will find information on the probate process, the records that were created, and ways of accessing them.

Probate is the process whereby the property of a decedent is distributed to his or her heirs. A person who dies "testate" (the testator) makes a will detailing his or her wishes as to that distribution. The making of a will must be witnessed by at least two disinterested persons who, after the decease of the testator, "prove" the will to a court as to its authenticity and the intent of the testator. This "proving" (also called probate) allows the estate to be administered by the executors — named by the testator — who oversee the distribution of the testator's estate according to his or her wishes, but also according to the law.

If a decedent dies without a will — dies "intestate" — and leaves property, an administrator is appointed to oversee the distribution of the decedent's estate according to the law.

Laws concerning inheritance have changed over time — at different times and places heirs were defined in different ways. This book explains how inheritance laws changed in New York and how those changes affected the records.

A glossary of basic probate terms is provided in order to understand the probate process.

Surrogate's Courts

The surrogate's offices for every county were canvassed concerning preservation of records and access to them. Each county page includes sections on Contact Information, Family History Library Microfilms, Published Records, and Online Records.

Contact Information

Pertinent dates in the county's history are found at the top, along with a map showing the location of the county in New York State. All addresses, phone numbers, and hours of operation are current as of Fall 2010. The physical address of the surrogate's court is given, as well as the mailing address if it is different from the physical address.

Because the surrogate's court is a state court, it may be closed on legal state holidays. In addition to federal holidays, New York courts observe state holidays, including Lincoln's and Washington's Birthdays (separately), Flag Day, and Election Day. Some of these holidays are not observed on the same day every year. Check with the court for possible closures prior to visiting.

Photocopy and research fees, which vary from court to court, may be sizable. Current state law allows the surrogate's court to charge $90 simply to locate a file. Photocopy fees of up to $6 a page for a certified copy are also allowed. Uncertified copies might cost as little as $.25 a page. Check the fees with the court prior to ordering photocopies. In some counties, older surrogate's records have been transferred to an archive or an historical society. These institutions usually charge significantly lower fees.

The surrogate will sometimes waive the search fee in some counties if provided with the exact name of the decedent, date of probate, and file number — all of which you can usually obtain by consulting the microfilmed index. Prior to ordering you might inquire if the fee will be waived

An alternative, but not always less expensive, option is to make a personal visit, or to hire a professional genealogist locally to go into the surrogate's court. The courts *usually* do not charge the search fee to walk-in requests, and sometimes not even the full copy fee. Before visiting in person, call ahead to confirm access and determine any restrictions or fees that may be in place. Some courts will pull files only at certain times of day or on certain days of the week.

Under a "new" directive from the Unified Court System, all counties are or will soon be scanning *new* files. In some counties, the images are available on computer and can usually be printed out from there. Some counties have also scanned older files.

If you are fortunate to be working in a county with an established county archive or county historian with an interest in record preservation, access to the original records may be easier. Ontario County, for example, has placed its surrogate's index on the Internet, and genealogists can order copies online. Because Ontario County probate packets are not on microfilm at the Family History Library, this is a benefit to the researcher.

Family History Library Microfilm

The Genealogical Society of Utah has microfilmed at least some original surrogate's records for all but four of New York's sixty-two counties and makes them available at the Family History Library (FHL) and its worldwide system of Family History Centers. Family History Centers are often, but not always, associated with a local Latter-day Saints church. Some public and private libraries are also included in the system. The New England Historic Genealogical Society, for instance, functions as a Family History Center. Researchers can order the films to be viewed there in Boston. For a description of this process (specific to New York), see Gordon L. Remington, "New York State Research through Family History Library Resources," *New England Ancestors* 3 (2002): 17–19.

Coverage varies for each county, but most counties have some records available to at least 1900. Bronx and Nassau Counties were formed at the turn of the twentieth century, and these records, like other modern records, were not filmed. Sullivan County experienced a devastating fire that destroyed its records. It is not known why the records of Suffolk County, one of the original New York counties, were not filmed.

This section of the county page indicates only those official county records on microfilm at the FHL, by type of record. The list is intended to be a general guide to the types of records available. More specific information on the records, dates covered, and individual film numbers can be obtained by consulting the FHL Catalog (FHLC) online at *www.FamilySearch.org*. In most cases, records for a specific county can be found using the "place name" search. Once the desired county is located in the FHLC, surrogate's records of all types can be found under the subject "Probate Records."

The FHL collection is not comprehensive, even for the pre-1900 period. It consists mainly of records in bound volumes, not collections of loose files. While the FHL has microfilm of *some* original surrogate's records for fifty-eight New York counties, its collection of probate packets or estate files is *not* complete for the entire state. The Family History Library has microfilmed some probate packets or estate files from twenty-four New York counties. Coverage varies, and not all counties have packets arranged alphabetically or chronologically. In all cases it is usually necessary to consult the surrogate's index to determine a file number.

For nearly every county there is a general index to surrogate's records extending well into the twentieth century, allowing researchers to determine the existence of an estate and to obtain a citation before writing to the county surrogate for records.

Published Records and Indexes

In addition to the microfilm collection at the Family History Library, published abstracts of many probate records have appeared in books, typescripts, and periodicals. You can find these published records in many genealogical societies, archives, and libraries with major genealogical collections. Those records available at FHL, NEHGS, and the New York Genealogical and Biographical Society Collection at the New York

Public Library, Library of Congress, New York State Library, and the National Society Daughters of the American Revolution Library are marked with an icon.

Microtext
FHL   ●FHL

Manuscripts/Published Works
DAR   ⫴DAR
FHL   ⫴FHL
LOC   ⫴LOC
NEHGS   ⫴NEHGS
NYPL   ⫴NYPL
NYSL   ⫴NYSL

The list includes typescripts and manuscripts as well as published works. Abstracts and transcriptions published in periodicals include the volume and page numbers to facilitate locating them. Appendix C at the back of the book discusses how to use published records.

Online Records

Many published and typescript abstracts and transcriptions of records have been published online.

Ancestry.com, for example, has published the *New-York Historical Society Collections* abstracts. Four major websites were examined for probate records.

The New England Historic Genealogical Society's website, *www.AmericanAncestors.org*, has several databases of New York probate records. The largest, Abstracts of Wills, Administrations and Guardianships in NY State, 1787–1835, comes from abstracts made by William Applebie Daniel Eardeley; it includes information from most counties. The database is described as follows:

> This compilation of Abstracts of New York Wills, Administrations and Guardianships was created by William Applebie Daniel Eardeley. The original materials are part of the Brooklyn Historical Society's manuscript collection. Eardeley abstracted original estate proceedings in the counties of this state. In addition he indexed on 3 x 5 cards all the names in his abstracts, i.e. those of the decedents, executors, administrators, petitioners, guardians, witnesses, named beneficiaries and minor children. The original abstracts were written in pencil on yellow legal pad paper. Although the original title of the collection refers to the years 1691 to 1860, the bulk of the material concerns the period 1787 to 1835. Also, while the abstracts generally end at 1835, it appears that in a few cases the dates were extended to fill a county's file folder. For estate proceedings of counties formed after 1835, the researcher should look under the names of the parent county.

The database is fully searchable for all names mentioned. Images of the original abstracts are linked to search results. In a few instances Eardeley's abstracts appear to have omitted information contained in the original records.

Sampubco, *www.sampubco.com*, has published indexes to testators for New York counties, and for a fee will retrieve a copy of the will. Many of the Sampubco indexes were originally published as individual book indexes for each county. While the printed Sampubco indexes contained will testators only, the online indexes have been expanded to include letters of administration, letters testamentary, guardianships and surrogate's records/probate files at the Family History Library. The last category gives the estate file numbers with which one can order copies of the probate packets. Sampubco will soon be adding dower records as well.

The USGenWeb Archives Project, *www.usgwarchives.org*, contains indexes, abstracts, and transcriptions of will and other probate matters, including Sampubco indexes and abstracts. Sampubco customers are encouraged to add abstracts of wills they obtain to the USGenWeb Archives Project. Select New York from the main page, then choose the county you wish to research.

Other websites, such as that of the Ontario County Department of Records and Archives (*http://raims.com*), are mentioned when they include valuable resources.

Appendixes

Three appendixes contain additional information for your research. Appendix A contains a list of all New York counties, including those that are now extinct. The chart includes date of formation, territory added to or ceded from the county, mother and daughter counties, and the county seat. Appendix B lists organizations that will be helpful to you in your research. Appendix C is a discussion about using published records and original records. Finally, a glossary lists important terms relevant to probate research in New York.

Understanding
New York State
Probate Records

Understanding New York State Probate Records

New York probate is a complex subject, even after the creation of the system of a Surrogate's Court for each county in 1787. Before 1787 there was probate in county courts and there was centralized probate in New York City for estates worth more than a certain amount. The key set of abstracts is *Abstracts of Wills on File in the Surrogate's Office, City of New York, 1665–1800*, 17 vols., Collections of The New-York Historical Society, vols. 25–41 (New York, 1893–1909). This set should always be searched, even though the abstracts are not always correct, especially in the earlier volumes. To the extent they survive, the original will liber and the original will should be reviewed (however, original wills have been filmed only up to about 1738). Four original will libers from this period have not survived, and if the will in question is from one of those four libers *and* the original will itself has not survived, then the nineteenth-century copy of the will libers should be reviewed.

Abstracted wills for New York are also to be found in Berthold Fernow, *Calendar of Wills on File and Recorded in the Offices of the Clerk of the Court of Appeals, of the County Clerk at Albany, and of the Secretary of State, 1626–1836* (New York: Colonial Dames of the State of New York, 1896; reprint Baltimore: Genealogical Publishing Co., 1967). The wills Fernow abstracted are in various collections, mostly in the New York State Archives.

The creation of the Surrogate's Court system in 1787 simplified probate in New York, but there were still inconsistencies and overlapping jurisdictions until 1829. In that year a new set of laws and rules improved the system and instituted the requirement of probate petitions naming the heirs at law, regardless of the provisions of the will (if there was one). These probate petitions are a valuable resource for New York research. The Family History Library has microfilms of probate packets (which include the petitions) from only about 40% of the counties in the state.

One of the most valuable online sources is "Abstracts of Wills, Administration and Guardianships of NY State, 1787–1835," a database on the NEHGS website, *www.AmericanAncestry.org*. It consists of handwritten abstracts of probate from almost every county in existence by 1835. This is particularly valuable for upstate New York research.

Many nuances affect research in New York probate, including the following:

- There are hundreds of wills in the New York State Archives (and elsewhere) that do not appear in either *Abstracts of Wills* or Fernow;

- Many wills were unrecorded — and they are still being discovered;

- Wills that were appealed may only have survived in the records of the appeals court;

- Wills may have been recorded at the town or county level, especially in deed books;

- Wills may have been recorded in a neighboring colony or state (e.g., Vermont, Massachusetts, Connecticut, or New Jersey) or in London; and

- Wills proved after 1787 may not have been recorded in the Surrogate's Court of the county of residence for a variety of reasons.

What New York State lacks in vital records it makes up for with its probate records. A wealth of genealogical information is contained not only in the standard wills and administrations, but also in ancillary records, and, most importantly, the petition required to probate or administer an estate after 1829.

Probate records in New York State are often referred to as "surrogate's records." New York is one of a few states and Canadian provinces where the officer in charge of probate records is called a surrogate—literally "one appointed to act in place of another." For genealogists the term helps to explain how probate records were kept in the colonial, Revolutionary, and post-Revolutionary periods.

Records were kept by a central authority from the earliest settlement through 1787. On 20 February of that year, the state legislature passed a comprehensive law dealing with the probate of estates and the keeping of related records. It is therefore useful to consider the pre–1787 records as a group, whether created under Dutch, British, or American rule.

Pre-1787 Records

There was no official probate court during the jurisdiction of New Netherland between 1624 and 1644. Records of wills and other estate matters can be found mixed with other provincial business and in the private records of notaries. No wills were recorded in the official registers at New York City during the seven-month period of the Dutch reoccupation of New York in 1673–1674. Matters of probate were presumably handled locally during this time.

From 1664 to 1787, almost all estates probated in the colony were recorded in the capital, New York City, by the New York County court. After 1787, *most* probate records will be found in the surrogate's court in the decedent's county of residence.

Unlike many other states, where the probate courts are the province of county government, the New York surrogate's courts remain state courts. Although many are physically located in county courthouses, the rules governing access to records and fees are dictated by the state. In some instances, a county clerk may have some probate records, both in registers of miscellaneous records and in miscellaneous loose papers.

The establishment of a state Court of Probates in 1778 affected most of upstate New York, with only that portion of Westchester County under British rule still directed by the Royal Governor until 1783. All probate records were kept at the state level between 1778 and 1787.

Most of the records in the colonial period have been transcribed, abstracted, or indexed, and they should be available in most libraries with major genealogical collections. Pre-1787 probate records are also available online in a variety of formats.

The most concise account of records in this era is "New York Probate Records Before 1787" by Harry Macy, Jr. (*The NYG&B Newsletter* 2 (Spring 1991): 11–15). An updated version of this article is available to members of the New York Genealogical and Biographical Society online at *www.newyorkfamilyhistory.org*. Macy's article includes a chart (Statewide Wills, Administrations, and Inventories Filed at New York City, 1665–1787) that provides a description of each type of record, where it is available, and any indexes and abstracts.

Post-1787 Records

On 20 February 1787, the state legislature passed a comprehensive law dealing with the probate of estates and the keeping of related records. The law, to take effect on 1 May of that year, created a state Court of Probates, with original jurisdiction over estates consisting of property in more than one county, and appellate jurisdiction over estates settled entirely within a single county. Original jurisdiction over estates settled entirely within one county was given to a surrogate in each county, who was also to maintain the records relating to such estates.[1]

This lasted until 1823, when the state Court of Probates was abolished. The power to probate estates was vested in the county surrogate. Appellate jurisdiction was now granted to the state Court of Chancery.

From 1786 to 1829, the state Supreme Court of Judicature and the county courts of common pleas held concurrent jurisdiction with the Court of Probates and the county surrogate's courts in matters of wills of real property, as well as those cases where witnesses were unable to appear in court. Wills proved in the Supreme Court at New York City (the lowest court in the state judicial system) between 1787 and 1829 are in the custody of the New York County Clerk. Wills proved before the Supreme Court

---

[1] Vosburgh, Royden W., "Surrogate's Courts and Records" p.108 [see p. 6]; *Laws of the State of New York Passed at the Sessions of the of the Legislature Held in the Years 1785, 1786, 1787 and 1788 Inclusive, being the Eighth, Ninth, Tenth, and Eleventh Sessions.* (Albany: Weed, Parsons, and Co., 1886), p. 421, Tenth Session, Chapter 38.

at either Albany (1799–1829) or Utica (1818–1829) are currently located at the state archives.[2]

In 1847, the state court system was overhauled. While the surrogate's courts in each county remained intact, the Court of Chancery was abolished and appellate jurisdiction was transferred to the state Supreme Court.

Wills proved in county courts of common pleas were recorded by the county clerk.

For a fuller treatment of organization, jurisdiction, and record keeping, see the following:

Daly, Charles P. *The Nature and Extent and History of the Jurisdiction of the Surrogates' Courts of the State of New York.* New York, 1863.

Folts, James D. *"Duely and Constantly Kept": A History of the New York Supreme Court, 1691–1847 and an Inventory of its Records (Albany, Utica, and Geneva Offices, 1797–1847).* Albany, N.Y.: New York State Court of Appeals and The New York State Archives and Records Administration, 1991.

Vosburgh, Royden W. "Surrogate's Courts and Records in the Colony and State of New York, 1664–1847." *The Quarterly Journal of the New York State Historical Association* 3 (1922): 105–16.

---

[2] Probate Records, New York State Archives Information Leaflet #3.

Timeline for New York Probate Records

1624–1644 New Netherland implements Roman-Dutch Law.

1665–1673 English conquest; The Duke's Laws implemented. Records of estates valued at more than £100 are sent to New York City.

1673–1674 New Netherland regains control; probate reverts to Roman-Dutch law.

1674–1691 England regains control; Duke's Laws reinstated.

1683–1686 Charter of Liberties; two witnesses to wills and dower rights of widows introduced.

1686–1689 Dominion of New England; governor of New York to oversee probate; records in Boston.

1689–1691 Leisler's Rebellion; James II deposed and Jacob Leisler serves as governor, overseeing probate.

1691–1778 Colonial Era; English rule restored; Prerogative Court established at New York City in 1691, all estates to be probated there. In 1692, delegates for outlying counties appointed to handle probate matters, but records forwarded to New York City. Local courts of common pleas in some counties allowed to probate estates valued under £50.

1778–1787 State Court of Probate created, replacing colonial governor and prerogative court. Council of Appointment now names county surrogates. Custody of all records held in New York City transferred to the secretary of state for New York in 1783.

1787–1823 County surrogates have original jurisdiction over estates within one county. State Court of Probate has original jurisdiction over estates in multiple counties. Supreme Court of Judicatures has concurrent jurisdiction.

1823 State Court of Probate abolished.

1829 Supreme Court of Judicature no longer has jurisdiction. Probates to include a petition with names of decedent, petitioner, and heirs-at-law.

1847 Court of Chancery abolished. Appellate jurisdiction transferred to state Supreme Court (the lowest state court).

New Netherland, 1624–1664, 1673–1674

Understanding Dutch Rules of Inheritance

The so-called Roman-Dutch Law, developed in the early seventeenth century by Grotius and other Dutch jurists, applied in New Netherland with some variations. A useful discussion of the background of probate law in New Netherland can be found in *Inheritance and Family Life in Colonial New York City* by David Evan Narrett (Ithaca, N.Y.: Cornell University Press, 1992). While Narrett's focus is on New York City, his study of colonial probate practice can generally be applied to the whole province. According to Narrett, Dutch inheritance laws were somewhat complex, but the important points can be summarized as follows:

Wills: In general, a testator could bequeath his or her property to anyone, but the blood relatives (called "heirs by law") of the testator retained certain rights to a guaranteed portion of the estate. The size of the portion depended on how many heirs there were and the degree of relationship.

A peculiar aspect of probate records during the Dutch period is that wills could be recorded while the testator was still living; therefore, there was no reason to prove them after the testator's death.

Mutual Wills: Under Roman-Dutch Law, a man and wife held property jointly. Because of this, the practice of making a mutual will, each party giving all property to the survivor, was common. In New Netherland, the surviving spouse generally maintained control over the family's assets, particularly when minor children were involved. Such wills were often recorded while the couple was living. Children, male and female, eldest and youngest, were generally considered to share equally in the property.

Intestate Estates: In general, the property was divided equally among the blood heirs of the decedent according to degrees of kinship. If a married person died intestate, the estate was divided in half: one half went to the surviving spouse; the other half was divided equally among the blood relatives of the decedent.

Guardianships: Officials called *orphanmasters* looked after the interests of minor children, even if one parent survived.

Records

Family History Library Microfilm

The Family History Library has the original of many of these records on microfilm under the heading "Court and Civil Records of New Amsterdam and New York, 1650–1895":

- Original minutes, orphanmasters court 1655–1668
- Minutes, orphanmasters court (cont.) 1644 [sic. 1655]–1668
- Register of Salomon Lachaire 1662–1664 (notary public)
- Dutch court records (English) v. 1–3, 1661–1749
- Wiltwyck/Kingston, v. 1–6, 1661–1684
- Kingston Secretary's papers, v. A–E, 1664–1681
- Kingston account books, 1676–1719, 1742, 1772–1774 (poor funds, deacons, and church records)
- Dutch court records (Dutch), v. 1–6, 1661–1686
- Secretary's papers, v. B, 1666–1680

Published Records

Original records during this period are, of course, written in Dutch, but through the efforts of various scholars and the Holland Society of New York, most pertinent records of estates have been translated into English and published. The following are chief among these publications. Please note that some are available online.

> Anjou, Gustave. *Ulster County, N.Y. Probate Records in the Office of the Surrogate, and in the County Clerk's Office at Kingston, N.Y.: A Careful Abstract and Translation of the Dutch and English Wills, Letters of Administration after Intestates, and Inventories from 1665, with Genealogical and Historical Notes, and List of Dutch and Frisian Baptismal Names with their English Equivalents.* New York: the author, 1906.[3] Online at Ancestry.com; digitized versions are available at GoogleBooks.com; HeritageQuestOnline.com; and the Internet Archive, *www.archive.org.*

> Christoph, Peter R., Kenneth Scott, and Kenn Stryker-Rodda. *Kingston Papers. New York Historical Manuscripts: Dutch* (volume 6 and 7 of). Baltimore: Genealogical Publishing Co., 1976.

---

[3] While his abstracts are generally considered accurate, Anjou's reputation for fraud should be taken into consideration when using this work, particularly in regard to his editorial comments. See Robert Charles Anderson, "We Wuz Robbed: The modus operandi of Gustave Anjou," *Genealogical Journal* 19 (1991): 47–58; Gordon L. Remington, "Gustave, We Hardly Knew Ye: A Portrait of Herr Anjou as a Jungberg," *Genealogical Journal* 19 (1991): 59–70; and Louise Hasbrouck Zimm, "Lieutenant Gysbert Crum of Espous, New York (Was he a Step-son of Jan Joosten Van Meteren?)," *The New York Genealogical and Biographical Record* 81 (1950): 197–202 at 202.

Fernow, Berthold, trans. and ed. *Minutes of the Orphanmasters of New Amsterdam, 1655 to 1663: Translated and Edited under the Auspices of the Committee of History and Tradition of the Colonial Dames . . . of New York.* 2 vols. New York: E. P. Harper, 1902.[4] Available online at GoogleBooks.com and at the Internet Archive, *www.archive.org.*

Gehring, Charles T. *Fort Orange Court Minutes, 1652–1660.* Syracuse, N.Y.: Syracuse University Press, 1990.

—————. *Fort Orange Records, 1656– 1678.* [Fort Orange eventually became Albany.] Syracuse, N.Y.: Syracuse University Press, 2000.

Gehring, Charles T., and Janny Venema. *Fort Orange Records, 1654–1679.* Syracuse, New York: Syracuse University Press, 2009.

Pearson, Jonathan. *Early Records of the City and County of Albany and Colony of Rensselaerswyck (1656–1675): Translated from the Dutch, with notes.* 4 vols. Albany, N.Y.: J. Munsell, 1869. [Vols. 3 and 4 in this series also begin during the New Netherland period; revised and edited by A.J.F. van Laer, and published 1918–19.] Available at GoogleBooks.com, HeritageQuestOnline.com, and the Internet Archive, *www.archive.org.*

Scott, Kenneth, and Kenn Stryker-Rodda. *The Register of Solomon Lachaire, Notary Public of New Amsterdam, 1661–1662: Translated from the Original Dutch Manuscript in the Office of the Clerk of the Common Council of New York by E. B. O'Callaghan. New York Historical Manuscripts: Dutch.* Baltimore: Genealogical Publishing Co., 1978.

Stryker-Rodda, Kenn, and Kenneth Scott, eds. *The Minutes of the Orphanmasters of New Amsterdam, 1663–1668: Translated from the Dutch by Edmund B. O'Callaghan.* Baltimore: Genealogical Pub. Co., 1976.

Van Laer, Arnold J. F. "Register of the Provincial Secretary, 1638–1660." *New York Historical Manuscripts: Dutch.* 3 vols. Baltimore: Genealogical Publishing Co., 1974.

—————. *Minutes of the Court of Albany, Rensselaerswyck, and Schenectady, 1668–1685,* 3 vols. Albany, N.Y.: University of New York, 1926–1932. Available online at Ancestry.com.

---

[4] Volume 1 contains the minutes of the orphanmaster; Volume 2 contains the "Minutes of the executive boards of the burgomasters of New Amsterdam and the records of Walewyn Van der Veen, notary public, 1662–1664." This work is available to NYGBS members online at *www.newyorkfamilyhistory.org.*

The English Period, 1665–1783

Different Categories of Laws during the English Period

The Duke's Laws, 1665–1673, 1674–1691

For the twenty-one years following the English conquest of New Netherland in 1664, New York was a proprietary province—the personal possession of James Stuart, the Duke of York—and governed by a code of laws popularly known as the "Duke's Laws." Drawn up in 1665 by the duke's representatives, these laws specified that the courts of session held jurisdiction over matters of probate. If an estate exceeded £100, the records relating to it were to be transmitted to the Secretary of the Province in New York City. It is possible, therefore, to find record of some estates in local courts of session. Some probate matters can also be found in the court of assizes, the highest court in the province.[5]

Between 1664 and 1683, English probate practices were not enforced in predominantly Dutch areas. Even so, English legal concepts, such as primogeniture and partible inheritance of personal property in cases of intestacy, were introduced. According to Narrett, this had the side effect of encouraging the Dutch population to safeguard all of their children's inheritances by making wills.[6]

The Charter of Liberties, 1683–1686

For eighteen years after the introduction of the "The Duke's Laws" in 1665, the Dutch population was allowed to use their customs. The Charter of Liberties and Privileges of 1683 was an attempt by the first colonial assembly to codify the various laws in the province.

With regard to inheritance, paragraph 21 of the charter stated "That From hence forward Noe Lands Within this province shall be Esteemed or accounted a Chattle or personall Estate but an Estate of Inheritance according to the Custome and practice of his Majestyes Realme of England," essentially introducing the rule of primogeniture (see below), which conflicted with the more egalitarian Dutch system of inheritance.

---

[5]   Royden W. Vosburgh, "Surrogates' Courts and Records in the Colony and State of New York, 1664–1847," *The Quarterly Journal of the New York Historical Association* 3 (1922): 105–16.

[6]   Narrett, pp. 129–130, 165–166.

Other matters of inheritance were addressed in paragraphs 24 and 25. Paragraph 24 specified "That All Wills in writing attested by two Credible Witnesses shall be of the same force to convey Lands as other Conveyances being registered in the Secretaryes Office within forty dayes after the testators death." This paragraph conflicted with the Dutch custom of recording wills before one's death. Paragraph 25 stated

> That a Widow after the death of her husband shall have her Dower And shall and may tarry in the Cheife house of her husband forty dayes after the death of her husband within which forty dayes her Dower shall be assigned her And for her Dower shall be assigned unto her the third part of all the Lands of husband dureing Coverture, Except shee were Endowed of Lesse before Marriage.

This paragraph established the dower right of widows and was essentially unchanged until abolished by the revised statute of 1829. After that, a widow had to be proactive in claiming dower.

The Dominion of New England, 1686–1689

When the Duke of York ascended the throne of England in 1685, New York became a royal colony. In 1686, James II disallowed the Charter of Liberties and declared that New York's laws would be the same as those in the newly created Dominion of New England. In 1688, he attached New York to the Dominion of New England.

In England, the power to probate estates was vested in various ecclesiastical courts. Ultimate jurisdiction lay with the Prerogative Court of the Archbishop of Canterbury, but the Commissary Court of the Bishop of London technically had power over ecclesiastical affairs overseas.[7] His 1686 instructions for the governance of New York, however, explicitly vested the power to probate estates in the colony's governor. In effect the business was handled by the secretary of the province, who was also described as the governor's principal *surrogate*.

During New York's brief union with the Dominion of New England (1688–1689), the secretary of the province appears to have continued to act as the surrogate of the governor, who was now in Boston. During this period, sixteen New York wills and administrations were recorded there, for which see Henry B. Hoff, "New York Probates Recorded in Massachusetts, 1688–1689, during the Dominion of New England," *The New York Genealogical and Biographical Record* 139 (2008): 269–73.

Leisler's Rebellion, 1689–1691

The Glorious Revolution of 1688 resulted in the deposition of James II and the dissolution of the Dominion of New England. A vacuum of power occurred in New York the following year. In order to prevent adherents of James from gaining control of the province, a popular rebellion catapulted Jacob Leisler, a minor military officer, to the

---

[7] Rex Maurice Naylor, "The Royal Prerogative in New York 1691–1775," *The Quarterly Journal of the New York State Historical Association* 5 (1924): 221–251, at 250.

position of de facto governor from 1688 to 1691, though the legitimacy of his government was imperfect. No wills probated under "Governor" Leisler were found in the New-York Historical Society abstracts.

Colonial Era, 1691–1778

After the suppression of Leisler's Rebellion in 1691, the English consolidated their rule and established the basic institutions that lasted throughout the colonial period. Although the Dutch population continued to preserve their inheritance customs, it was a period of anglicization: English customs and laws eventually prevailed. A prerogative court was established in New York in 1691. Originally all estates were to be probated at New York City. In 1692, however, the initial business of settling estates in counties remote from New York City was delegated to officers variously known as deputies, delegates, or surrogates. The records were still to be forwarded to the Prerogative Court in New York City, which had final authority to grant probate. In some counties, the local court of common pleas was empowered to grant probate on estates valued at under £50. If no appeal was made to the Prerogative Court, the only records relating to such an estate should be found in the records of those local courts. This distinction applied only to the counties of Dutchess, Ulster, and Albany until 1750, when Orange was granted the same privilege. The counties of Tryon (Montgomery) and Charlotte (Washington) were granted the privilege soon after their formation in 1772.[8]

Revolutionary Era, 1778–1787

The State of New York was established in 1778, but the British did not fully withdraw from New York until November 1783. On 16 March 1778, the new state legislature passed an act organizing the government. One provision of this act established the judge of the state Court of Probates as having the same authority previously vested in the British governor and Prerogative Court to oversee estates. Surrogates in each county were now to be named by the Council of Appointment. The county surrogates continued to forward the records to the central court. Estates in that part of Westchester County, as well as New York City and Long Island, still under occupation of the British continued to be probated in New York City.[9]

After the end of the Revolution and the evacuation of the British from New York, all probate authority rested with the state Court of Probates. Custody of all records held in New York City was transferred to the secretary of the State of New York on 21 November 1783.[10] This was the last time they would be intact for almost two hundred years.

According to New York State Archives Information Leaflet #3, "Probate Records":

---

[8] Ibid., p. 107. The counties of Gloucester and Cumberland (now in Vermont) were also granted this privilege in 1772.

[9] Vosburgh, p. 107.

[10] William S. Pelletreau, "Abstracts of Wills on File in the Surrogate's Office, City of New York" *Collections of the New-York Historical Society for 1900,* vol. 33.

The pre-1787 records of the former Prerogative Court and the Court of Probates were divided in 1802: original wills and other filed papers relating to the "Southern District" (New York, Kings, Queens, Suffolk, Richmond, and Westchester Counties) and all record books were transferred from Albany to the New York County Surrogate's Court. (The records sent to New York City included series J0038-92 and J0043-92. . . .) Other filed papers of the Court of Probates remained in Albany. After the court was abolished, the Albany records passed into custody of the Secretary of State (1823–29), the Court of Chancery (1829-47), and the Court of Appeals (1847+). These records were placed on deposit at the Historical Documents Collection, Queens College, CUNY, in 1973, and transferred to the State Archives in 1982 and 1985.

The story of the records' peregrinations between New York City and Albany is of academic interest only to the extent that it explains why different printed sources covering the same records indicate that the records are in different repositories, depending on the date of publication. For genealogical purposes it is only important to know that the originals of these province- and state-level records can be found at the New York State Archives in Albany or the Surrogate's Court of the County of New York in New York City. Copies on microfilm are located at the New York Public Library in New York City and the Family History Library in Salt Lake City.[11] Family History Library films are available for loan through its worldwide system of Family History Centers.

Rules of Inheritance during the English Period

English Rules of Inheritance, 1665–1690

Wills: Major changes between Dutch and English probate are twofold. First, wills were to be probated and recorded after death. Second, women no longer retained an equal right to property—their legal standing being that of a "femme covert." Any property a woman might possess at marriage or inherit after marriage became that of her husband, unless explicitly indicated otherwise.

Intestate Estates: The English common law concept of *primogeniture* in estates of real property appears to have been introduced with the 1665 Duke's Laws; it was explicitly adopted in the Charter of Liberties in 1683.[12] Generally stated, the eldest son would inherit all real property. If there were no sons, then real property would be divided equally between any surviving daughters. If there were no children at all, then real property would descend to the oldest male heir, possibly a brother or nephew.[13]

The Duke's Laws introduced a system of *partible inheritance* for personal property, whereby the widow would receive one-third, with the remaining property divided equally

---

[11] A concise account of the history of the custody of the pre–1787 records can be found in Kenneth Scott, *Genealogical Data from New York Administration Bonds 1753–1799 and Hitherto Unpublished Letters of Administration* (New York: The New York Genealogical and Biographical Society, 1969), pp. 1–3.

[12] Narrett, pp. 127–128.

[13] See John Frederick Dorman, "Colonial Laws of Primogeniture," 1969 World Conference on Records, Salt Lake City, published as a leaflet (Salt Lake City: Genealogical Society of Utah, 1969), I–12.

among the children of the deceased (the eldest son receiving a double portion). This was in conformance with the system in place in New England, and it is likely that in the English parts of New York this practice persisted until at least 1691.

Royal Province Rules of Inheritance, 1691–1783

Wills: Disposition of property continued to be at the discretion of the testator.

Intestate estates: The descent of real property continued to be governed by primogeniture.

The Statute of Distributions of 1670 (22–23 Charles II), which governed the descent of personal property in England, ostensibly applied in the province after 1691. An intestate's wife received one-third of the personal estate, and the remainder was divided equally among his children, except that the share of any child, other than the heir-at-law, who received a settlement or advance in the lifetime of the intestate, would be reduced until all shares were of equal value. In 1774 the New York Assembly passed "An Act for the Better Settling of Intestates Estates," officially codifying the Statute of Distributions into provincial law.[14]

There is some disagreement among legal scholars and historians as to the extent to which the Statute of Distributions was accepted after 1691. The consensus seems to be that it was assumed to apply and thus gained acceptance by usage; however, the possibility remains that some estates continued to be settled according to Dutch custom and/or the Duke's Laws.

Records

Despite the confusion of the last two centuries resulting from questions of jurisdiction and custody, the original pre-1787 probate records of New York State are now located in one of two places: the New York State Archives in Albany or the Surrogate's Court of the County of New York.

The *register* copies of wills originally kept by the New York County Surrogate's Court consist of two sets. The original set is missing volumes 4, 7, 9, 18, and 28. The second set, a transcription made in the nineteenth century, is complete. Original libers 1–2, 3–4, 5–6, 14–14A, and 30–31 were combined into single volumes with new pagination, making perseverance a necessity when locating a will. All other volumes were given a unique pagination for the transcription, noting the original page number in the margin.

---

[14] *The Colonial Laws of New York from the Year 1664 to the Revolution, Including the Charters to the Duke of York, the Commissions and Instructions to Colonial Governors, the Duke's Laws, the Laws of the Dongan and Leisler Assemblies, the Charters of Albany and New York and the Acts of the Colonial Legislatures from 1691 to 1775 Inclusive*, 5 vols. (Albany, N.Y.: James B. Lyon, 1894), 5: 614–18. Narrett, p. 127, states that the Act of 1774 merely made the Statute of Distributions official, while Dorman states that it excluded altogether children who had received advances. A comparison of the Act of 1774 with the 1670 Statute shows that Narrett is correct.

Microfilm copies of the original will liber set and the second set are available in the New York Genealogical and Biographical Society Collection at the New York Public Library, and the New York State Library, as well as through the Family History Library. The second set of libers are at the New York County Surrogate's Court. The New-York Historical Society has a duplicate of the second set of will libers, made through a nineteenth-century photographic process.

In addition to reviewing the register copy of the will, one should also consult the original, or "holographic," copy if available. There is always the chance that the register copy contains an error, and the original may contain annotations that weren't copied into the registers. The register copy, however, will contain the date of probate and other official notations that may not be on the original.

Because of the various removals of records from one repository to another, original records were separated at one point. For a time they were deposited at Queens College in Flushing, where they were organized and assigned numbers. It was this collection that was microfilmed in 1967 by the Genealogical Society of Utah to about the year 1738.

Besides wills, numerous other records relating to estates survive from the colonial period. Administrations prior to 1743 were included in the will libers and in the New-York Historical Society abstracts. After 1743, they were kept separately. This is reflected in the abstracts as a simple list giving the name of the intestate, the name of the administrator, and the date letters were issued or granted. The original volumes of Letters of Administration after 1743 are in the custody of the Surrogate's Court of the County of New York.

In addition, some ancillary records relating to the probate of estates in colonial New York have survived. In some cases these records supplement what is in the registers; in other cases, new information is provided.

New York State Archives

New York State Archives Information Leaflet #3, "Probate Records," contains succinct descriptions of each type of probate record held by the state archives, indicates whether or not it has been microfilmed, and notes existing finding aids and indexes for each.[15] The descriptions below are from this publication. Fuller descriptions and detailed historical background on these records can be found by consulting the online catalog of the Archives at *www.archives.nysed.gov/a/research/res_topics_legal_probate.shtml*.

J0043–92 Probated Wills, 1665–1787 (38 vols.)

Abstracts of wills and grants of administration; many wills predating 1700 are in Dutch with English translations. Series also contains estate inventories and accounts of administrators (pre-1708); and letters of administration (pre-1743). Volumes also contain some non-probate records, including scattered entries of marriage licenses, ca. 1684–1706.

---

[15] The 1994 version of this leaflet is available online at *www.archives.nysed.gov/altformats/GuidesHistRecs/ prob-fact.txt*. Updated information is available through the archives' online catalogue.

J0038–92 Probated Wills, 1665–1787

Original wills and scattered other documents relating to probate of wills and administration of estates. Most but not all testators resided in New York City, Long Island, Staten Island, or Westchester County.

This series is organized into two sub-series: 1) ca. 1658–1738; 2) ca. 1739–1787. There are copies of many of these wills in series J0038–82. Wills are arranged by an assigned file number, with separate numbering sequences for the two sub-series; some numbers are missing from each sub-series. Many original wills are missing; however, J0038–92 includes some unrecorded wills not found in J0043-92. Researchers may be advised to first look at the recorded probate records before requesting to look at a original will. Since the pre–1738 wills have been microfilmed, any restrictions apply only to the original wills in sub-series 2.

JU0038–82 Probated Wills, 1671–1815 (11 microfilm rolls)[16]

Wills (most in English, some in Dutch) and a few letters of administration and property inventories. Most of the testators resided north of Westchester County. Many of the wills are copies of wills in series J0038–92. Arranged by assigned alphanumeric file number. Documents are stable but fragile; use microfilm.

⬤FHL   The FHLC reference to these wills is misleading, for it lists them under Albany County even though they apply to the entire state.

Catalogued under:

NEW YORK, ALBANY—PROBATE RECORDS
[For FHLC film/fiche search, use FHL 481435]

Catalogued as:

New York. Surrogate's Court (Albany County). Record of wills proved at Albany, New York, 1629–1802; index 1629-1828. (Salt Lake City : Filmed by the Genealogical Society of Utah, 1967.) 13 microfilm reels.

The FHLC assigns the original will files letters AA through AZ. In order to correlate the assigned alphanumeric file number listed in Fernow to the correct FHL film on which to find the original will, simply delete the letter A. Thus, the will for Rudolphus Swartwout, which was listed as 1584 (**S 113**) by Fernow, is found on FHL film #481444, described in the FHLC as containing: "Wills, **AS 113**–AU 1629–1802"

There is also a card index to the entire series on FHL 481435 item 2 that may be useful in converting from Fernow's published abstracts to the FHL films.

---

[16] These are the original wills abstracted by Fernow in his *Calendar of Wills* (see Published Records below). The original records abstracted by Kenneth Scott and James A. Owre can be found in several collections at the New York State Archives and the Family History Library.

J0301–82 Inventories and Accounts, 1666–1822 (7 microfilm rolls)

Inventories of personal property and accounts of decedents' debts and credits, prepared by administrators and executors. Most of the inventories and accounts relate to estates located north of Westchester County. Arranged in three subseries, 1666–1699, 1700–1775, and 1776–1822, and thereunder alphabetically.[17]

> ●FHL   The FHLC reference to these wills is again misleading, for it lists them under Albany County when they apply to the entire state.
>
> Cataloged under:
>
> NEW YORK, ALBANY—PROBATE RECORDS
>
> Cataloged as:
>
> New York. Surrogate's Court (Albany County). Original records of administrations of estates, 1700–1825, and inventories and accounts, 1600s–1700s. (Salt Lake City : Filmed by the Genealogical Society of Utah, 1967.) 22 microfilm reels. [For FHLC film/fiche search, use FHL 504477.]
>
> *Note:* The 22 reels of FHL microfilm apparently correspond to both New York State Archives series J0301-82 and J0033-82. The only direct correlation that can be made, however, is between the first two subseries of J0301-82:
>
> 1666-1699 = Inventories of estates, 1600s
> (FHL 504477/501472)
>
> 1700–1775 = Inventories, 1700s
> (FHL 509056-509057, 501473)
>
> The Family History Library Catalog then lists three further series:
>
> Admin[istration] 1700-1775 (6 reels plus card index)
> Admin[istration] & inventory 1776–1825 (4 reels plus card index)
> Admin[istration] & inventory 1776–1825 (6 reels plus card index)

J1301-04 Estate Inventories, ca. 1730-1753 [1 roll microfilm (part)]

Contents: Original inventories of estates; documents were filed in New York City but relate to estates in many parts of the province. Several indexes to groups of inventories are included in the microfilm.

J2301-04 Record of Estate Inventories, 1779–1786 [1 roll microfilm (part)]

Contents: Volume contains inventories of estates recorded by the clerk of the Court of Probates. Index at end of volume.

> ●FHL   New York. Surrogate's Court (New York County) Inventories, v. Q-3 - Q-4 1730-1786. (An FHLC film/fiche search for 478746 will return this series in the results.)

---

[17]   The first two sub-series are indexed in Scott's "New York Inventories, 1666–1775."

J033–82 Administration Papers, ca. 1700–1823 (17 microfilm rolls)

Series contains letters of administration, performance bonds of administrators and executors, renunciations of executorships, accounts of administrators and executors presented to the court, property inventories, court orders, and other documents relating to administration of estates. Arranged alphabetically by decedent.

J090 Orders in Chancery 1701–1708, 1720–1770 (4 vols.)

This series consists mainly of copies of orders and decrees issued by the Royal Governor or Lieutenant Governor acting in his capacity as Chancellor. The first three volumes, covering 1701 to 1735 contain summary information. The fourth volume, containing records between 1748 and 1770, includes minutes of court proceedings that give detailed information about the cases.

J0065 Chancery Decreees and Papers before 1800, 1684–1815 (4 vols.)

This record group contains information on the particulars of cases, the results of court investigations, the content of testimony, and the determinations of the court. The records consist of decrees, bills of complaint, answers, testimonies, reports, and other documents filed in cases heard by the Chancellor. Information content varies depending on the documents filed for each case.

J059 Chancery Minutes 1781–1829 (47 vols., 18 microfilm rolls)

Daily records of the proceedings of the Court of Chancery. Information includes the names of the parties and their attorneys, summaries of arguments and documents read or submitted, and actions taken by the court.

New-York Historical Society *Collections*

Between 1892 and 1904, the New-York Historical Society published 17 volumes of abstracts of wills proved between 1665 and 1800 as part of their *New-York Historical Society Collections* series. The abstracts in volumes 1–9 and in volume 11 were made by William S. Pelletreau. Those in volume 10 were made by Rev. John Keller. The abstracts in volumes 12 to 14 are not credited. The second half of volume 14 and all of volume 15 continue with New York County will libers 40–42 (1787–1800). Volumes 16 and 17 are corrections to the earlier volumes.

Prior to 1743, many types of probate records are included in the abstracts, because all business of the Prerogative Court was recorded in the same volumes. Records of administration were kept separately after 1743. This is reflected in the abstracts as a simple list giving the name of the intestate, the name of the administrator, and the date letters were issued or granted.

Except for the original, unrecorded wills in volume 11, the wills on which these abstracts are based are the *register* copies originally kept by the New York County Surrogate's Court.

It is not certain which set Pelletreau used for his abstracts, and it is possible that he looked at both. He used the new pagination for volumes 1–8, 10, and 19B, indicating that for those abstracts, at least, he was using the second set. All other volumes have the original pagination, but since the second set contains both, it is impossible to know if he ever consulted the originals. Pelletreau was supposed to have done much of his work from them.[18] If Pelletreau used the "second set" or a poor copy of it, his abstracts are third or fourth hand. While the second set is more complete, the first set should be consulted whenever possible.

Table 1 indicates which libers are included in each volume. The Arabic numerals refer to the overall *New-York Historical Society Collections* volume. The Roman numerals indicate the serial volume number for wills within the N-YHS collections.

TABLE 1

Volume 25 [I]	**1665–1707**	Libers 1–7 (to p. 484/*358*)
(1892)		Appendix: "wills translated . . . from the Dutch after the foregoing copies were made; . . .original wills not recorded, but on file in 'Bundle No. 1,' Surrogate's office; . . . early wills which were recorded in later books"
Volume 26 [II]	**1708–1728**	Libers 7 (p. 484/*358* to end), 8–10, 14A, 19B
(1893)		Appendix: "includes some wills not on record, and also wills and documents in Liber 19B"
Volume 27 [III]	**1730–1744**	Libers 11–15 (to p. 199)
(1894)		Appendix A: Letters of Administration 1744
		Appendix [B]: Complaints of Court of Mayor and Alderman in Liber 19B
Volume 28 [IV]	**1744–1753**	Libers 15 (p. 199 to end)–18
(1895)		Appendix: Dutch language wills (translated) and Letters of Administration Granted November 16, 1745 to March 19, 1753
Volume 29 [V]	**1754–1760**	Libers 19–22 (to p. 214)
(1896)		Appendix: Corrections and Letters of Administration issued from May 1, 1753 to September 27, 1760

---

[18] Comments of Harry Macy, Jr., FASG, when reviewing this text.

Volume 30 [VI]	**1760–1766**	Libers 22 (p. 216 to end)–25 (to p. 226)
(1897)		Letters of Administration Issued from September 3, 1760, to December 29, 1766; Corrections
Volume 31 [VII]	**1766–1771**	Libers 25 (p. 229 to end)–28 (to p. 128)
(1898)		Letters of Administration Granted from January 6, 1767 to 1773; Appendix (apparently additions and corrections); Errata
Volume 32 [VIII]	**1771–1773**	Libers 28 (p. 131 to end)–30
(1899)		Letters of Administration Granted from January 13, 1773, to January 15, 1779; Addenda, Corrections
Volume 33 [IX]	**1773–1783**	Libers 31–33
(1900)		Letters of Administration Granted from January 17, 1773, to February 18, 1783
Volume 34 [X]	**1780–1782**	Libers 34–35 (to p. 148)
(1901)		
Volume 35 [XI]	**Pre–1790**	Unrecorded Wills Prior to 1790
(1902)		
Volume 36 [XII]	**1782–1784**	Libers 35 (p. 151 to end)–37 (to p. 184)
(1903)		Letters of Administration Granted July 20, 1782, and from February 5, 1783, to December 31, 1784
Volume 37 [XIII]	**1784–1786**	Libers 37 (p. 185 to end)–39 (to p. 127)
(1904)		Letters of Administration Granted from January 11 to December 30, 1785
Volume 38 [XIV]	**1786–1787**	Liber 39 (p. 127 to end)
(1905)		Letters of Administration Granted from January 5, 1786, to December 31, 1795[19]

---

[19] This volume is fully imaged on GoogleBooks, the only volume of the series that can be viewed and downloaded as a PDF.

Volume 39 [XV]   **1796–1801**   Libers 42–43

(1906)   Letters of administration Granted from January
                                    4, 1796 to December 30, 1800

Volume 40–41 [XVI–XVII]   Corrections, Volumes I–XI (i.e. 25–35)[20]

(1906)

Table 2 displays original will libers keyed to New York will abstracts. The Dates column
indicates the inclusive dates for each original liber. Dates in [brackets] indicate where the
description of the inclusive dates for a particular "second set" volume is in error. Original
volumes 1 and 2 are combined in the "second set" volume for 1665–1699.

Table 2

Original Will Libers Keyed to New York Will Abstracts

(T) = volume of the "second set" (N-YHS abstracts); (O) = volume of the original will libers

Original Libers	Dates	FHL #	19th-century "Second Set"	FHL #	N-YHS Vol.
Lib. 1	1665–1683	907920	1665–1699[83]	874513	25 (T)
Lib. 2	1682–1699	497592	(1&2)		
Lib. 3	1684–1694	497592	1684–1687[93]	874514	25 (T)
Lib. 4	missing		(3&4)		
Lib. 5	1698–1699	497593	1693–1707	874515	25 (T)
Lib. 6	1703–1707	497593	(5&6)		
Lib. 7	missing		1702–1704	874516	25 (T)
Lib. 8	1710–1716	497593	1710–1716	874517	26 (T)
Lib. 9	missing		1718–1724	874518	26 (O)
Lib. 10	1724–1728	497593	1724–1728	874519	26 (T)
Lib. 11	1730–1732/3	497593	1730–1732/3	874520	27 (O)
Lib. 11	p. 307	497594			
Lib. 12	1732/3–1736	497594	1732/3–1736	874521	27 (O)
Lib. 13	1736–1741	497594	1736–1741	874522	27 (O)
Lib. 14	1740–1742	497594	1740 [1688]–1765	874523	27 (O)
Lib. 14A	1687–1765	497592	(14&14A)		26 (O)
Lib. 15	1742–1746	497595	1742–1746	874524	27/28 (O)

---

[20]   Because these wills are abstracts from the original records, mistakes were made; it is always wise to check
these volumes for corrections.

Original Libers	Dates	FHL #	19th-century "Second Set"	FHL #	N-YHS Vol.
Lib. 16	1746–1749	497595	1746–1749	875149	28 (O)
Lib. 17	1749–1751	497595	1749–1751	875149	28 (O)
Lib. 17	p. 106 to end	497596			
Lib. 18	missing		1751–1754	875150	28 (O)
Lib. 19	1754–1756	497596	1754–1756	875150	29 (O)
Lib. 19B	1680–1687	497592	1680–1687	875151	26 (T)
Lib. 20	1756–1758	497596	1756–1758	875151	
Lib. 21	1758–1760	497596	1758–1760	875152	29 (O)
Lib. 21	p. 482 to end	497597			
Lib. 22	1760–1761	497597	1756–1761	875153	29/30 (O)
Lib. 23	1761–1763	497597	1761–1763	875154	30 (O)
Lib. 24	1763–1764	497597	1762[63]–1763[64]	875155	30 (O)
Lib. 24	p. 499 to end	497598			
Lib. 25	1765–1767	497598	1765–1767	875156	30/31 (O)
Lib. 26	1767–1769	497598	1767–1769	875157	31 (O)
Lib. 27	1769–1771	497598	1769–1771	875158	31 (O)
Lib. 27	p. 572 to end	497599			
Lib. 28	missing		1771–1773	875159	31/32 (O)
Lib. 29	1773–1775	497599	1772[73]–1775	875160	32 (O)
Lib. 30	1774–1776	497599	1767[74]–1768[78]	875161	32 (O)
Lib. 31	1776–1778	497599	(30&31)	875161	33 (O)
Lib. 32	1776–1778	497600	1778–1780	874774	33 (O)
Lib. 33	1778–1783	497600	1778–1782[83]	866984	33 (O)
Lib. 34	1780–1782	497600	1780–1782	866985	34 (O)
Lib. 35	1782–1783	497600	1782–1783	866986	34/36 (O)
Lib. 35	p.238 to end	484023			
Lib. 36	1783–1784	484023	1780[82]–1784	866987	36 (O)
Lib. 37	1784–1785	484023	1784–1785	866988	36/37 (O)
Lib. 38	1785–1786	484023	1785–1786	866989	37 (O)
Lib. 39	1786–1787	484023	1784[86]–1787	866990	37/38 (O)
Lib. 39	p. 100 to end	493478			

Family History Library Microfilm

Wills

New York. Surrogate's Court (New York County). Record of Will Libers, New York City, 1662–1927.[21]

New York. Surrogate's Court (Albany County). Record of wills proved at Albany, New York, 1629–1802; index 1629–1828.[22]

Administrations

Letters of Administration, 1743–1866; index, 1743–1910. New York. Surrogate's Court (New York County).[23]

New York. Surrogate's Court (Albany County). Original records of administrations of estates, 1700–1825, and inventories and accounts, 1600s–1700s.[24]

New York. Surrogate's Court (New York County). Administration bonds, 1753–1866.[25]

Guardianships

New York. Chancery Court. Chancery Minutes and Orders, 1701–1847.[26]

———. (New York County). Minutes of the Court of Chancery, 1711–1847; Supreme Court trial term, 1939–1942.

———. Index to Chancery Court Records, 1700–1848.[27]

---

[21] Film number 501142 contains original wills and index for the years 1662–1761.

[22] The FHLC assigns the original will files letters AA–AZ. Delete the initial letter A to correlate the assigned alphanumeric file number listed in Fernow to the correct original will on the FHL film. For example, the will for Rudolphus Swartwout, which was listed as 1584 (S 113) by Fernow, is found on FHL film no. 481444: "Wills, AS 113–AU 1629–1802" FHL film no. 481435, item 2, has a card index to the entire series that may also be useful in converting from Fernow's published abstracts to the FHL films.

[23] An FHLC Film/Fiche search for 872170 will return this collection.

[24] An FHLC Film/Fiche search for 504477 will bring up this collection. These 22 reels of microfilm apparently correspond to New York State Archives series JO301–82 and JO033–82. The only direct correlation that can be made, however, is between the first two subseries of JO301–82: 1666–1699 = Inventories of estates, 1600s (FHL 504477/501472); 1700–1775 = Inventories, 1700s (FHL 509056–509057, 501473).

[25] This record group contains bonds in volumes B–I, covering the years 1753–1798. An FHLC search for 907917 will show this series.

[26] Minutes, orders, and proceedings for the years 1701–1702, 1705–1708, 1720–1735, 1740 [sic, actually 1748]–1770 are found on FHL No. 017439. Minutes for the years 1781–1808 are found on FHL No. 017418–422.

[27] An FHLC search for film No. 1204888 will bring up these records.

Published Records

"Abstracts of Wills on File in the Surrogate's Office, City of New York." *Collections of the New-York Historical Society*, Vols. 25 to 39, 1892–1904. (See a detailed explanation of these abstracts at p. 19.)

Barber, Gertrude Audrey. "Index to Letters of Administration of New York County, from 1743–1875." Typescript, New York [?]: 1951.[28] ●FHL

Fernow, Berthold. *Calendar of Wills on File and Recorded in the Offices of the Clerk of the Court of Appeals, of the County Clerk at Albany, and of the Secretary of State*. New York, 1896; Reprint, Baltimore: Genealogical Publishing Co., 1967.[29]

Bloch, Julius M., Leo Hershkowitz, and Kenneth Scott. "Wills of Colonial New York, 1736–1775." *National Genealogical Society Quarterly* 54 (1966): 98–124.

Kelly, Arthur C. M., comp. *Index, Names of Principals: Abstracts of Wills 1665–1776 on File in the Surrogate's Office City of New York—Abstracts Published by the New York Historical Society Collections 1892–1899*. New York: New York Historical Society, 1892-1899; Reprint, Rhinebeck, N.Y.: Palatine Transcripts, 1981.[30]

————. *Index, Names of Principals: Abstracts of Wills 1777–1800 on File in the Surrogate's Office City of New York—Abstracts Published by the New York Historical Society Collections 1900–1906*.[31] New York: New York Historical Society, 1900-1906; Reprint, Rhinebeck, N.Y.: Palatine Transcripts, 1981.

New York Abstracts of Wills, 1665–1801, CD-ROM. Bowie, Md.: Heritage Books, 1997.[32]

Sawyer, Ray C., comp. *Index of Wills for New York County (New York City), from 1662–1850*. Typescript. n.p.: 1930. ●FHL

---

[28] Barber includes state/province wide administration prior to 1787. She listed the name of intestate, the name of the administrator, the date the letters were granted/recorded, and the volume and page where they are recorded.

[29] Fernow states that his calendar brings to light many wills of New York City, Westchester County, and Long Island. He made his abstracts from a number of different sources, not all of which were "original" pre–1787 wills. In all cases he gave the source of the will he was abstracting. He assigned his abstracts a sequential number from 1 to 2162. When his abstract was of an original will, it was correlated to an alphanumeric file number consisting of the first letter of the decedent's surname and a number in that alphabetical sequence. For example, the will of Rudolphus Swartwout is listed by Fernow as abstract #1584 correlated to original will file (S 113). It is important to note that the index to Fernow refers to is his abstract number, not the page number or the alphanumeric file number.

[30] This index refers only to the name of the decedent and uses the volume number for the series (1–17).

[31] This index refers only to the name of the decedent and uses the volume number for the series (1–17).

[32] This CD-ROM contains the images of each page of the original New-York Historical Society series, plus a master-index to the entire series. The master index uses the serial volume numbers (1–17). You can search for a name wherever it occurs in the entire series and consult a facsimile of the printed volumes.

Scott, Kenneth. "Early Original New York Wills." *National Genealogical Society Quarterly* 51 (1963): 90–99, 174–78, 185.[33]

—————. *Genealogical Data from Administration Papers from the New York State Court of Appeals in Albany.* Middletown, N.Y.: The National Society of Colonial Dames in the State of New York, 1972.

—————. *Genealogical Data from New York Administration Bonds 1753–1799 and Hitherto Unpublished Letters of Administration.* New York: New York Genealogical and Biographical Society, 1969.[34]

—————. "New York Inventories, 1666–1775." *National Genealogical Society Quarterly* 54 (1966): 246–59.

—————. *Records of the Chancery Court Province and State of New York: Guardianships 1691–1815.* Middletown, N.Y.: The Holland Society of New York, 1971.

Scott, Kenneth, and James A. Owre. *Genealogical Data from Inventories of New York Estates 1666–1825.* New York: New York Genealogical and Biographical Society, 1970.

Online Records

Ancestry.com

New York County, Letters of Administration Index, 1743–1875 (Barber Collection) (same as Barber above).

New York City Wills, 1665–1707, 1706–1709, 1708–1728, 1730–1744, 1744–1758, 1754–1760, 1760–1766, 1766–1771, 1771–1776, 1777–1783, 1780–1782.[35]

New York Wills, 1626–1836 (same as Fernow above).

---

[33] Records cover the period from 1665 to about 1738. The original wills 1 through 1204 listed by Scott, plus will number 1205, are available on FHL film numbers 501142–501147. The catalog entry states that these original wills cover the years 1662–1761, but reference to Scott's article indicates that only six wills in this series date later than 1738.

[34] This book covers three different collections of records housed in three different places. The original administration bonds from 1753 to 1799 are at the New York County Surrogate's Court and on microfilm at New York State Archives. Four volumes (two each of letters of administration for 1788–1790 and 1791–1799 and two each of administration bonds for 1787–1791) were in the Historical Documents Collection at Queens College when Scott abstracted them. Only the latter are now in the custody of the State Archives. The others were not located at the county surrogate's court or the NYC Municipal Archives.

[35] These are the same as the Pelletreau abstracts published by the New-York Historical Society. The introductions to the databases suggest that all the "wills" are for residents of New York City and do not explain that they also apply to residents of the entire province and that probate matters other than wills are included. While the online abstracts use the page numbers from the original New-York Historical Society abstracts, it does not give the serial volume numbers (1–17), so it is difficult to inspect the printed volumes and/or to go from the online abstracts to the original wills.

Estates Probated in England

As previously stated, ultimate authority to probate estates in the pre-Revolutionary period rested in the Prerogative Court of the Archbishop of Canterbury (PCC). Not surprisingly, with commercial and military activity occurring in the province, a number of New York estates were recorded in that court. PCC wills can also be searched (by testator, date, place, and occupation) online at *www.nationalarchives.gov.uk/documentsonline*.

The estates of Americans probated in the PCC have been abstracted in three works by Peter Wilson Coldham:

> *American Wills & Administrations in the Prerogative Court of Canterbury, 1610–1857.* Baltimore: Genealogical Publishing Co., 1989.

> *American Wills Proved in London, 1611–1775.* Baltimore: Genealogical Publishing Co., 1992.

> *North American Wills Registered in London, 1611–1857.* Baltimore: Genealogical Publishing Co., 2007.[36]

A study of these two volumes reveals the estates of at least fifty-seven New York residents recorded in the PCC between 1683 and the Peace of 1783. Of these, some twenty-nine were military or naval officials. Even after 1783, however, wills of New York residents were still being probated in the PCC. Some of these were for British military personnel who made their wills while still in New York (causing them to be described as "of New York"), but who died after the British evacuation in 1784. In addition, the estates of a number of New York Loyalists who removed to England were probated in the PCC.

Abstracts of estates of Americans probated in England at the PCC and elsewhere can be found in two series in the *New York Genealogical and Biographical Record*, as follows:

> J. Henry Lea and J. R. Hutchinson. "Clues from English Archives Contributory to American Genealogy," *NYGBR* 40 (1909): 80–86, 177–85, 229–40; 41 (1910): 4–9, 72–82, 183–91, 278–86; 42 (1911): 92–100, 168–76, 294–301, 430–34; 43 (1912): 27–73; 44 (1913): 116–24.

> Lothrop Withington. "New York Gleanings in England." *NYGBR* 34 (1903): 288–91; 35 (1904): 119–22, 179–84, 271–76; 36 (1905): 22–36, 114–18, 172–76, 260–63; 37 (1906): 49–53, 184–878; 38 (1907): 205–06; 39 (1908) 46–50, 217–19.

These series were included in Henry B. Hoff. *English Origins of American Colonists from the New York Genealogical and Biographical Records* (Baltimore: Genealogical Publishing Company, 1991).

---

[36] This volume is an abridged version of the previous two volumes.

New York State, 1778–Present

In 1778, New York State formally declared its independence from Great Britain and drafted a constitution. New Yorkers living in areas occupied by the British (New York City, Long Island, and part of Westchester County) continued to be governed by the probate laws of the Royal Province until 1783. New Yorkers living in the independent state of New York were governed by new laws. Depending on location and date, probate has been handled by one of four types of bodies:

- Court of Probates, 1787–1823
- Supreme Court of Judicature, 1786–1829
- Court of Chancery, 1777–1847
- Secretary of State's Office, 1823–1966

After a discussion of rules of inheritance, this section will address where to find records of each of these courts.

Understanding Rules of Inheritance

Wills: The testator continued to have complete discretion over the disposition of property. Married women were given the right to own their own property in 1848, after which a married woman was allowed to leave wills disposing of that property even if she predeceased her husband.[37]

Intestate Estates: On 12 July 1782, primogeniture was abolished and replaced with a new system for the descent of real property.[38] Real property descended first to a person's "heirs at law" (a person's lawful issue) in equal shares. If a child or other descendant predeceased a parent, his or her share would be further divided among his/her issue if any survived. In the absence of lineal descendants, the property would descend to

---

[37]   Sessions Laws of New York, 1848, Chapter 200.

[38]   "An Act to abolish entails, to confirm conveyances by tenants in tail, to distribute estates real of intestates, to remedy defective conveyances to join tenants, and directing the mode of such conveyances in future," *Laws of the State of New York Passed at the Session of the Legislature Held in the Years 1777, 1778, 1779, 1780, 1781, 1782, 1783 and 1784, Inclusive* (Albany, N.Y.: Weed Parsons and Company, 1886), 1: 501–502, Sixth Session, Chapter 2. Indeed, Robert Clinch of Schenectady, in his will dated 10 September 1781 and probated 21 December 1781, stated "I leave my eldest son, Ralph, one Spannish Milled Dollar, wherewith he must be satisfied, *and make no further pretence or demand to any part of my estate by right of Primogeniture*," New York County Wills, Liber 33, p. 272.

the decedent's full-blood siblings. By 1865, half-siblings were allowed to share in the real property. That provision already existed for personal property. Half-siblings did not inherit property that came to the decedent by inheritance from a relative not shared by the half-sibling.[39] The descent of personal property was defined by the act of 20 February 1787, which basically adopted the English Statute of Distributions of 1670.

Heirs-at-Law

Beginning in 1830, state law required that all heirs-at-law be notified of the probate of will or the administration of an estate. This law applied even if the heirs-at-law to a testate estate were not mentioned in a will. This provision bears striking similarity to the Roman-Dutch provision guaranteeing a portion of the estate to the "heirs by law" of the testator, although no such guarantees are made. The probate petition, in New York a document of incredible value, is usually found among the loose probate papers relating to an estate.

Statewide Records

Between 1778 and 1787, all estates were probated in the state Court of Probates. The wills were grouped together with the provincial wills in New York City and are part of that collection at the State Archives in Albany. After 1787, records were maintained in various courts at the state level and in the individual county surrogate's courts. These records for the state-level courts are available at the New York State Archives in Albany, and many of them are also on microfilm in Salt Lake City.

Reference to the State Archives Series J0038–92 [original wills] and Series J0043–92 [registered wills] in the section on "Colonial and Pre–1787 Probate Records" above provide details on the nature and accessibility of these records (see p. 15). The Genealogical Society of Utah has not microfilmed the original wills in Series J0038–92 but has microfilmed the registered wills in Series J0043–092. These records are available at the Family History Library.

Court of Probates, 1787–1823
New York State Archives

J0043–85 Record of Wills and Probates 1787–1822 (2 vols.)

Wills registered by the Court of Probates, for which the court had granted letters of administration. Most wills were proved before a county surrogate or other judge.

J0032–83, –85 Letters of Administration 1778–1823

Letters of administration for estates of New York residents who died out of state, or nonresidents who died in the state. Most of the letters are for estates of persons who died intestate (without a will). (The first volume of this series, commencing 1778, as

---

[39] The Civil Code of the State of New York (Albany, N.Y.: Weed, Parsons, & Co., 1865), p. 191, Title VI, Section 657.

well as five volumes of administration bonds, 1787–1823, have not been transferred to the Archives.)[40]

J0039–85 Exemplification of Wills and Letters of Administration, 1783–1801 (1 vol.)

Official transcripts of wills, codicils, and letters of administration registered by Court of probates.[41]

J0020–82 Orders and Decrees, 1811–1823 (1 vol.)

These records concern administration of estates of out-of-state residents as well as non-residents dying in New York and appeals to the Court of Probates from the Surrogate's Courts. (Indexed by name of decedent and type of proceeding.)

●FHL Family History Library Microfilm

New York. Probate Court. Wills, 1787–1822. (This series was abstracted by Fernow and referenced as Volumes 1 and 2.)

New York. Probate Court. Letters of administration, 1778–1787. (This volume actually ends in 1797. It is not clear whether or not this volume corresponds to the first volume of Series J0032–83, –85. An FHLC film/fiche search for 017412 will return this series.)

New York. Probate Court. Letters Testamentary, 1793–1806. (The title board says "New York Probate Records Vol. 1 1793–1801," but the first letters in this volume were issued in 1783 and the last in 1801, so it is clear that this is the same volume described in NYSA J0039–85. An FHLC film/fiche search for 017417 will return this series.)

J0039-04 Record of Letters Testamentary, 1793-1801 [1 roll microfilm]

Letters testamentary were issued by the Court of Probates when the executor designated in a will was unable to perform the duties of the office. Index to testators at front of volume.

These records are not at the Family History Library.

J0042-04 List of Wills and Other Documents Delivered by the Judge of the Court of Probates to the Surrogate of the City and County of New York, 1799 [1 roll microfilm]

Roughly chronological list of wills that were transferred to the New York County Surrogate's Court when the Court of Probates removed its office to Albany in 1799. Each entry gives name of testator, residence, and date of will. Wills relate only to estates located within the First Senatorial District (New York and adjacent counties); the wills

---

[40] Scott's works on records of administration indexes only the volumes for the years 1787–1799 (see p. 32).

[41] This series was abstracted by Fernow and referenced as Volume 3.

date from ca. 1662 to 1786. At the end of the main list are other lists of documents transferred, such as inventories, accounts of administrators, etc.

These records are not at the Family History Library.

Supreme Court of Judicature, 1786–1829
New York State Archives

J0041-82 Record of Wills Proved at Albany, 1799-1829.

Wills and probates (proceedings to determine authenticity of will). Volume is fragile. A few related documents concerning proof of wills in Supreme Court, including petitions for proof of will, affidavits of witnesses, and notices to heirs, are found in series J1041–82 Petitions and Affidavits for Proof of Wills (Albany), 1801–28.

J0020-82 Record of Wills Proved at Utica (1 vol.)

Wills probated in the state Supreme Court of Judicature at Utica, 1799–1829.

> **⊙FHL**   New York. Supreme Court. Wills, 1799–1829. (An FHLC film/fiche search for 017414 will return this series.)

New York. Supreme Court (Oneida County). Wills tried before Supreme Court at Utica, 1820–1829.[42]

J2041-04 Record of Wills Proved at New York, 1787-1829 [1 roll microfilm]

Two volumes of recorded wills and probates (summary of proceedings to determine authenticity of will). Original record is in the New York County Clerk's Office.

> **⊙FHL**   New York. Supreme Court (New York County) Wills, v. A–B, Dirk Sefferts, 25 Jan. 1787–Augustine Hicks Lawrence, 4 May 1829. (An FHLC film/fiche search for 501136 will return this series.)

Court of Chancery, 1777–1847

Between 1830 and 1847, the Court of Chancery shared with the Surrogate's Courts the power to prove wills when the testator or the witnesses resided out of state.

---

[42] The FHLC reference to these wills is misleading. It lists them under Oneida, Chenango, and Cayuga Counties when they actually apply to the entire state. An FHLC film/fiche search for 017413 will return this series.

New York State Archives

J0040–82, –85 Record of Foreign and Out-of-State Wills Proved, 1830–1848 (3 vols.)

Contains record of wills and proceeding in proof of wills. Some original wills, as well as documents relating to these proceedings (e.g., depositions) are found in J0057 *In Re* Papers.

> ●FHL   New York. Chancery Court. Wills of Real Estate, v. 1–3, 1830–1847. (The description of these wills in the FHLC does not mention "foreign" or "out of state," but examination of the microfilm showed that this is the same set of records as J0040–82, –85 above. An FHLC film/fiche search for 017415 will return this series.)

Secretary of State's Office
New York State Archives

B0081 Letters of Administration and Copies of Wills of Out-of-State Residents, 1823–1966[43]

Certified copies of wills and letters of administration, arranged by file number, for estates of out-of-state residents owning property in New York, and a small amount of correspondence. Some documents are fragile. There is no index; the file number or exact date of filing is required for retrieval.

Miscellaneous Records

In 1971, Kenneth Scott published "Genealogical Data from Further New York Administration Bonds" as volume XI of the *Collections of the New York Genealogical and Biographical Society*. He states there that two more volumes "from the Court of Appeals in Albany, containing bonds for the years 1791–1795 and 1795–1798 have been deposited in the Historical Documents Collection of Queens College of the City University of New York" since his 1969 publication of *Genealogical Data from New York Administration Bonds 1753–1799 and Hitherto Unpublished Letters of Administration*. These bonds deal almost exclusively with estates in New York City or out of state residents.

The Queens College collection was microfilmed by the Genealogical Society of Utah in 1967, before these volumes were deposited there. They are not on microfilm at the Family History Library. A diligent search failed to identify their present location.

County Clerk Records

Wills proved in county courts of common pleas between 1786 and 1829 were recorded by the county clerk. Each clerk maintains a set of "Miscellaneous Records" that encompass some probate records from this time period. The Family History Library

---

[43]   These records have *not* been microfilmed by the Genealogical Society of Utah.

has "Miscellaneous Records" from many New York counties, but they are catalogued inconsistently. Sometimes they are catalogued under "New York—[County Name]—[Court Records]" and sometimes under "New York—[County Name]—[Probate Records]." It was not practical to examine every set of "Miscellaneous Records" for each New York county at the Family History Library for inclusion in the Surrogate's Courts section of this book, so researchers should check these records if the desired estate is not found in the Surrogate's Court prior to 1829.

County Surrogate's Courts, 1787–present

The surrogate in each county is responsible for keeping records relating to the probate of both testate and intestate estates. In addition to the work by Daly and Vosburgh cited earlier, background information on the county surrogate's courts can be found in the following:

Macy, Harry, Jr. "Library Resources for Research in New York Probate Records Since 1787." *NYG&B Newsletter* 10 (1992): 3–7.

Arneson, John. "The Legal Angle in the Surrogate's Office." *Tree Talks* 3 (1963): 7–9.

Lapiana, John C. "New York State Surrogate Court Records." *Genealogy Tomorrow* 2 (1985): 3, 14–15.

Records

Bound surrogate's court records can consist of will registers, letters testamentary, letters of administration, accounts, appraisals, minutes, dower proceedings, orders, decrees, bonds, etc. The Genealogical Society of Utah has microfilmed at least some original records for all but four of the sixty-two New York counties. The missing counties are Bronx, Nassau, Suffolk, and Sullivan.

Most of these records are the same as those in most probate courts. Dower proceedings deserve special mention as a discrete set of records dealing with a widow's right to her one-third interest in the real estate held in common with her husband (known as "widow's thirds"). Not only do these records contain information concerning the exact portion of the estate set off to the widow, but they may also mention children or other heirs of the decedent.

Loose surrogate's court records are usually found in probate packets, estate files, or estate papers. Loose papers can include the original will, letters, administrators' and executors' bonds, accounts, newspaper notices to heirs, and related records.

The petition to probate or administer an estate is the single most important document in a post-1830 probate packet. The purpose of the petition is to protect the rights of all heirs-at-law, whether or not there was a will, and whether or not an heir-at-law was mentioned in a will. It was possible for a will to be contested, and it was necessary for the surrogate's court to have a list of heirs-at-law if that eventuality occurred.

The petition was supposed to give the following information:

- Name and residence of the decedent
- Date of death of the decedent
- Whether testate or intestate
- Name and relationship of the petitioner
- Names of the heirs-at-law, and their relationship to the decedent
- Residences of heirs-at-law, if known
- Ages of minor heirs (sometimes)

The list of heirs-at-law sometimes begins with "your petitioner" without repeating the name given in the preamble, so it is important to note the person presenting the petition.

There is some variation in the amount of detail given in the list of the heirs-at-law. In some cases, the names of deceased children are provided. Grandchildren may be listed, but the name of their parent may not be included. The record might also simply state that a named son or daughter is deceased and that the heirs are his or her children, but not give the names of such children. When a bachelor or single woman died intestate, the heirs-at-law might include nieces and nephews and even grand-nieces and nephews. Some probate petitions list cousins of varying degrees. Thus these petitions have the potential to provide a wealth of information on several generations of a family residing in a variety of locations.

There are cases where the petitioner, who usually lived near the decedent and was quite frequently a close relative, was unaware of the current residence of an heir-at-law who had relocated. In such cases the residence might be prefaced by "last heard of in" or "last known." Because the petitioner may be unaware of the death of such an heir, children of the heir would not be listed in the petition.

If the original petition cannot be located, other avenues may need to be used. In some counties (such as Chautauqua), the petition was recorded in books as well as filed in a packet. Since the purpose of the petition was to safeguard the right of all heirs-at-law, an additional requirement was to have a notice to all heirs-at-law published in a local newspaper advertising the fact that the estate had been admitted to probate. This notice contained the essential information given in the petition.

Details on accessing post-1787 records are provided in the Surrogate's Courts section of this book, which follow.

Surrogate's Courts

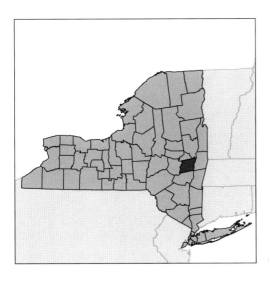

Albany County

Albany County Surrogate's Court[1]

30 Clinton Avenue
Albany, NY 12207

Date Formed	1 November 1683
County Seat	Albany
Parent County	Original

Phone   (518) 285–8585
Fax   (518) 462–0194
email   None
Hours   open to the public M–F 8:30–4:00
Website   www.nycourts.gov/courts/3jd/surrogates/albany/index.shtml

---

Records on Microfilm at the Family History Library

Records		Indexes	
Wills	1787–1901	Surrogates	1787–1959
Letters Testamentary	1856–1900		
Orders Probate of Wills	1868–1900		
Administrations	1794–1902		
Orders – Admin	1868–1901		

Published Records and Indexes

"Albany Probate Records: 1787–1796." Typescript.

Central New York Genealogical Society. *Tree Talks*. Syracuse, N.Y., 1961–.
█FHL █NEHGS █NYPL █NYSL

Wills	1734–1763
	6: 156; **7**: 20

---

[1] Surrogate's Court records from 1805 to 1958 are at the Albany County Hall of Records and may be used there with permission from the Surrogate's Office.

Administrations   1794–1810
4: 69, 122, 178; 5: 10, 59, 113, 164; 6: 13, 66, 108, 156;
48: 77–78; 49: 13–14, 77–78

Conway, Martin D., comp. *Index to Wills and to Letters of Administration: Index to Wills from 1780 to December 1, 1895, Index to Administrations from 1794 to December 1, 1895.* Albany, N.Y.: James B. Lyon, 1895.

Cook, William Burt, trans. *Abstracts of Albany, New York, Probate and Family Records.* Washington, D.C.: Library of the National Society of the Daughters of the American Revolution, 1930.

Hulslander, Laura Penny. "Abstracts of Deeds and Wills of Albany County, New York, 1768–1771." Typescript, 1992. ∥NYSL

Melius, Wheeler B. *Index to the Public Records of the County of Albany, State of New York, 1630–1894.* Albany: Argus Co. Printers, 1902–17 [indexed under wills, as if wills were a surname].

Nagle, Eric C. "Abstracts of the Wills of the County of Albany, State of New York, 1787–1800." Typescript, 1979. ∥NYSL

Van Laer, Arnold J. F., and Jonathan Pearson. *Early Records of the City and County of Albany and Colony of Resselaerswyck*, 4 vols. Albany, N.Y.: University of the State of New York, 1869–1919. ∥NYPL ∥NYSL

Online Records

New England Historic Genealogical Society
www.AmericanAncestors.org
Abstracts of Wills, Administrations and Guardianships in NY State, 1787–1835 [database].

Sampubco
www.Sampubco.com
Albany County wills from 1629 to 1836 are indexed.

This is a reference to Berthold Fernow, *Calendar of Wills on File and Recorded in the Offices of the Clerk of the Court of Appeals, of the County Clerk at Albany, and of the Secretary of State. New York, 1626–1836* (Orig. Pub. New York: Colonial Dames of the State of N.Y., 1896; reprint, Baltimore: Genealogical Publishing Co., 1967), which includes statewide wills archived in Albany.

County only wills are indexed for 1691–1900 and are still in process.

US Genweb Archives Project
www.usgwarchives.org
Includes the Sampubco indexes (above) as well as abstracts of Intestate Records, Letters of Administration, Letters Testamentary, Court Contests, and Estate Appraisals.

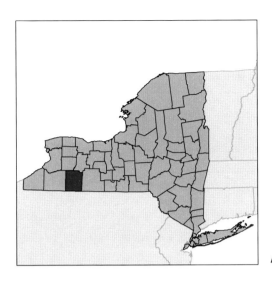

Allegany County

Allegany County Surrogate's Court

7 Court Street
Belmont, NY 14813–1084

Phone	(585) 268–5815
Fax	(585) 268–7090
email	None
Hours	M–F 9:00 am to 5:00 pm (Sep–May)
	M–F 8:30 am to 4:00 pm (Jun–Aug)
Website	www.nycourts.gov/Courts/8jd/Allegany/index.shtml

Date Formed	7 April 1806
County Seat	Belmont
Parent County	Genesee

Records on Microfilm at the Family History Library

Records

Wills	1831–1906
Letters Testamentary	1852–1901
Letters Administration	1852–1901
Guardian Orders	1852–1905
Guardian Books	1829–1884
Guardian Bonds	1890–1920
Final Settlement	1852–1904
Administration Bonds	1890–1900
Administration Orders	1869–1902
Orders, Minutes, & Decrees	1806–1903
Probate of Wills	1840–1865
Real Estate	1843–1899
Journal	1818–1884
Administration/Misc. Orders	1842–1886
Final Settlements	1885–1891

Indexes

Surrogates	1807–1952
Special Guard.	1884–1902

Published Records and Indexes

Central New York Genealogical Society. *Tree Talks*. Syracuse, N.Y., 1961–.
*f*FHL *f*NEHGS *f*NYPL *f*NYSL

Probate of Wills	1849–1864
	38: 85–86; **39**: 19–20, 83–84; **41**: 19–20, 83–84; **43**: 19–20;
	44: 19–20, 83–84; **45**: 15–16, 79–80; **46**: 15–16, 79–80;
	47: 15–16
Letters Test.	1831–1839
	30: 84, 149–150; **31**: 21–22; **32**: 84; **33**: 83; **34**: 21–22,
	85–86; **35**: 21–22
Estates	1807–1831
	3: 13; **4**: 20, 70, 123, 179; **5**: 114, 165; **6**: 67, 109, 157
Guardianships	1839–1864
	22: 89–90; **23**: 85–86; **24**: 21–22, 87; **32**: 83–84; **35**: 22,
	83–84; **36**: 21–22, 83–84; **37**: 21–22, 83–84; **38**: 21–22
Dower	1842–1879
	13: 138–39; **14**: 21; **18**: 149–50; **21**: 87–88
Misc. Proceedings	1826
	32: 22

Samuelsen, W. David. *Allegany County, New York, Will Testators Index, 1836–1906*. Salt Lake City: Sampubco, 1992. *f*NYSL

Records on the Internet

New England Historic Genealogical Society
www.AmericanAncestors.org

Abstracts of Wills, Administrations and Guardianships in NY State, 1787–1835 [database].

New York GenWeb, Allegany County
www.usgenweb.org

Includes some will indexes and abstracts.

Sampubco
www.Sampubco.com

Allegany County wills from 1795 to 1888 are indexed.
Guardianships from 1829 to 1895 are indexed.

US Genweb Archives Project
www.usgwarchives.org

Includes the Sampubco indexes, as well as abstracts of Intestate Records, Letters of Administration, Letters Testamentary, Court Contests, and Estate Appraisals.

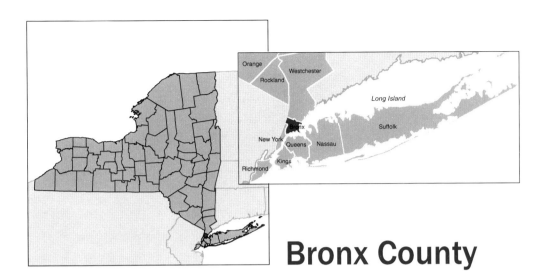

Bronx County

Bronx County Surrogate's Court

851 Grand Concourse, Room 317
Bronx, NY 10451–2937

Phone	(718) 618–2300
Fax	(718) 537–5158
email	None
Hours	M–F 9:00 am to 5:00 pm
Website	www.nycourts.gov/courts/12jd/index.shtml

Date Formed	19 April 1912
County Seat	Bronx
Parent County	New York

Special Notes

Files prior to 1950 are kept in the basement and require a three–day notice for retrieval. Small estates for 1964–1988 are on microfiche.

Wills and letters of administration are contained in annual or biannual volumes. All estates are supposed to be indexed on computer, but it is wise to also check the indexes in each volume.

Records on Microfilm at the Family History Library

None

Published Records and Indexes

None

Records on the Internet

None

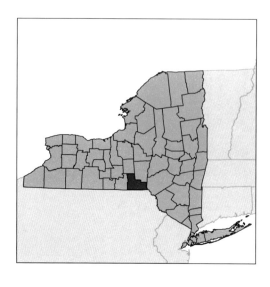

Broome County

Broome County Surrogate's Court
92 Court Street
Binghamton, NY 13901–3301

Mailing Address
Broome County Surrogate's Court
Broome County Courthouse
PO Box 1766
Binghamton, NY 13902

Phone	(607) 778–2111
Fax	(607) 778–2308
email	None
Hours	M–F 9:00 am to 5:00 pm
	M–F 8:00 am to 4:00 pm (Memorial Day to Labor Day)
Website	www.nycourts.gov/courts/6jd/Broome/surrogate.shtml

Date Formed	28 March 1806
County Seat	Binghamton
Parent County	Tioga

Records on Microfilm at the Family History Library

Records		Indexes	
Wills	1806–1906	Surrogates	1806–1951
Letters testamentary	1860–1912		
Executors Orders & Decrees	1871–1901		
Letters of Administration	1879–1912		
Admin. Orders & Decrees	1879–1897		
Judicial Settlement of Estate	1874–1902		
Guardianships	1830–1917		
Orders Appointing Guardians	1867–1917		
Dower Records	1830–1861		
Letters, Orders, & Decrees	1851–1879		
Minutes, Orders, & Decrees	1806–1933		

Records (cont.)

Miscellaneous Records   1863–1908
   (County Clerk)

Published Records and Indexes

Card, Lester L. "Broome County Surrogate Records, 1811–1843, vol. B–D."
   Typescript. ●FHL

Central New York Genealogical Society. *Tree Talks.* Syracuse, N.Y., 1961–.
   *FHL *NEHGS *NYPL

> Wills and Letters Test. 1806–1841 (ongoing)
> **15**: 27–28, 181–82; **16**: 85–86, 155–56; **17**: 77–78, 137–38;
> **18**: 21–22, 87–88; **19**: 23–24, 87–88; **20**: 25–26, 89;
> **26**: 17–18, 81–82; **45**: 82; **47**: 17–18, 81–82; **48**: 17–18,
> 81–82; **49**: 15–16, 79–80

Woodward, Mrs. Gordon H., abst. "Will Books, [1827–1850]," 3 vols. Typescript, n.d.
   ●FHL

Records on the Internet

New England Historic Genealogical Society

www.AmericanAncestors.org

> Abstracts of Wills, Administrations and Guardianships in NY State, 1787–1835
> [database].

Sampubco

www.Sampubco.com

> Broome County wills from 1795 to 1888 are indexed.
> Guardianships are indexed, dates not given (in progress).

US Genweb Archives Project

www.usgwarchives.org

> Includes the Sampubco indexes as well as abstracts of Intestate Records, Letters of
> Administration, Letters Testamentary, Court Contests, and Estate Appraisals..

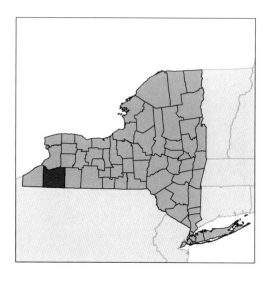

Cattaraugus County

Cattaraugus County Surrogate's Court

303 Court Street
Little Valley, NY 14755
Phone   (716) 938–2327
email   cwrona@courts.state.ny.us
Fax   (716) 938–6983
Hours   M–F 9:00 am to 5:00 pm
Website   www.cattco.org/court_system
           www.nycourts.gov/courts/8jd/Cattaraugus/index.shtml

Date Formed	11 March 1808
County Seat	Little Valley
Parent County	Genesee

Records on Microfilm at the Family History Library

Records		Indexes	
Wills	1830–1916	Surrogates	1800–1956
Letters Testamentary	1850–1904		
Letters Administration	1820–1901		
Administration Bonds	1890–1905		
Guardian Bonds	1890–1912		
Guardian Records	1830–1916		
Guardian Letters	1870–1902		
Judicial State	1885–1902		
Minutes, etc.	1847–1936		
Miscellaneous Records County Clerk	1817–1903	Misc	1800–1911

Published Records and Indexes

Central New York Genealogical Society. *Tree Talks.* Syracuse, N.Y., 1961–.
▮FHL ▮NEHGS ▮NYPL ▮NYSL

Wills	1830–1854
	9: 214; **10**: 27, 88; **11**: 23–24; **13**: 142–43; **14**: 25–26;
	22: 153, **28**: 25–26, 87; **33**: 25–26; **34**: 25–26; **35**: 25–26;
	36: 25–26; **37**: 25–26; **38**: 25–26; **39**: 23–24; **40**: 23–24;
	41: 23–24; **42**: 23–24; **43**: 23–24; **44**: 23–24; **45**: 19–20;
	46: 19–20; **47**: 19–20; **48**: 19–20
Letters of Admin.	1821–1829
	32: 25–26
Guardianships	1830–1855
	5: 62, 116, 167; **10**: 88, 152, 213; **11**: 23; **23**: 88; **24**: 25–26;
	25: 31–32

Samuelsen, W. David. *Cattaraugus County, New York Index to Will Books, 1830–1888.* Salt Lake City: Sampubco, 1991. ▮NYPL

———. *Cattaraugus County, New York, Will Testators Index, 1830–1916.* Salt Lake City: Sampubco, 1995. ◑FHL ▮FHL

Stahley, Susan E. *Cattaraugus County, New York, Surrogate Court Abstracts: Guardianship Edition.* Westminster, Md.: Heritage Books, Inc., 2008. ▮NEHGS

Western New York Genealogical Society. *Western New York Genealogical Society Journal.* Hamburg, N.Y., 1974–. ▮FHL ▮NEHGS ▮NYPL ▮NYSL

Surrogate's Index to 1892	
	28: 150–67; **29**: 17–27, 74–83, 122–27, 171–77; **30**: 28–35,
	61–73

Records on the Internet

New England Historic Genealogical Society
www.AmericanAncestors.org

Abstracts of Wills, Administrations and Guardianships in NY State, 1787–1835 [database].

Sampubco
www.Sampubco.com

Cattaraugus County wills from 1830 to 1916 are indexed.

Cayuga County

Cayuga County Surrogate's Court
153 Genesee Street
Auburn, NY 13021

Phone   (315) 253–1570
Fax   (315) 255–4324
Email   mmarr@courts.state.ny.us
Hours   M–F 8:30 am to 4:30 pm
Website www.nycourts.gov/courts/7jd/cayugacourts/surrogates

Date Formed	8 March 1799
County Seat	Auburn
Parent County	Onondaga

Cayuga County Records Management
12 Court Street
Auburn, NY 13021

Phone   (315) 253–1037
Fax   (315) 253–1036
Email   ccrecords@co.cayuga.ny.us
Hours   M–F 9:00 am to 5:00 pm (Sep–Jun)
         M–F 8:00 am to 4:00 pm (Jul–Aug)
Website http://co.cayuga.ny.us/records/recordslist.html

Special Notes

Cayuga County Records Management has records from 1799 through 1996. Later records are at the courthouse.

Records on Microfilm at the Family History Library

Records		Indexes	
Wills	1799–1904	Surrogates	1799–1952
Administrations	1802–1903		

Records (cont.)

Letters Testamentary & Admin.	1830–1902
Letters Administration	1876–1903
Records of Guardians	1804–1905
Records of Guardian Bonds	1890–1905
Guardians Orders	1877–1901
Surrogate Records/Prob. Packets	1799–1905

Published Records and Indexes

Barber, Gertrude A., comp. *Abstracts of Wills of Cayuga County, New York, 1799–1842.* 4 vols. ●FHL ▮NEHGS ▮NYSL

Card, Lester L., comp. "Cayuga County, New York, Surrogate Records, 1799–1815. Vol. 'A–1." Typescript, South Norwalk, Conn., 1930. ●FHL ▮NYSL

Central New York Genealogical Society. *Tree Talks.* Syracuse, N.Y. 1961–. ▮FHL ▮NEHGS ▮NYPL ▮NYSL

Wills	1799–1813
	21: 153; **32**: 28, 87, 149–50; **33**: 27–28, 87–88, 149–50; **34**: 27–28, 147–48; **35**: 27–28, 85–86, 147–48; **36**: 27–28, 85–86, 147–48; **37**: 27–28, 85–86; **46**: 83–84, 143–44; **47**: 21–22, 83–84, 143–44; **48**: 21–22, 83–84, 143–44; **49**: 17–20, 81–82, 143–44
Letters Test./Admins.	1830–36
	30: 90, 155–56; **31**: 27–28, 85–86, 149–50; **32**: 27–28; **37**: 149–50; **38**: 27–28, 87–88, 147–48; **39**: 25–26, 85

"Early Cayuga County, New York Wills, 1799–1809 from the Surrogates Office in Auburn, New York." Typescript, n.d.

Records on the Internet

Cayuga County Courthouse

http://co.cayuga.ny.us/records/recordslist.html
Surrogate's Court Records 1799–1996.

New England Historic Genealogical Society

www.AmericanAncestors.org
Abstracts of Wills, Administrations and Guardianships in NY State, 1787–1835 [database].

Sampubco

www.Sampubco.com
Cayuga County wills from 1799 to 1802 are indexed.
Guardianships from 1804 to 1852 are indexed.
Surrogate File Groups from 1800 to 1830 are indexed (in process).

US Genweb Archives Project

www.usgwarchives.org

Includes the Sampubco indexes as well as abstracts of Intestate Records, Letters of Administration, Letters Testamentary, Court Contests, and Estate Appraisals.

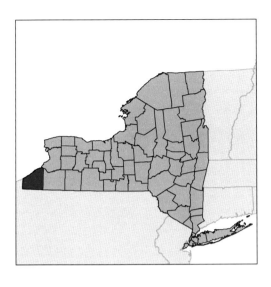

Chautauqua County

Chautauqua County Surrogate's Office

Gerace Office Building Courthouse
3 N. Erie St.
PO Box C
Mayville, NY 14757

Phone	(716) 753–4339
Fax	(716) 753–4600
email	lromer@courts.state.ny.us
Hours	M–F 9:00 am to 5:00 pm (Sep–May)
	M–F 8:30 am to 4:30 pm (Jun–Aug)
Website	www.nycourts.gov/courts/8jd/chautauqua/surrogates.shtml

Date Formed	11 March 1808
County Seat	Mayville
Parent County	Genesee

Special Notes

Probate petitions are in Probate of Wills books. They are also available on microfilm.

Records on Microfilm at the Family History Library

Records		Indexes	
Wills	1830–1900	Surrogates	1811–1962
Letters Testamentary	1841–1903		
Appointment of Appraisers	1841–1915		
Administration, Wills	1870–1911		
Letters of Administration	1818–1907		
Administrator Bonds	1871–1902		
Proceeding of Administration	1842–1901		
Guardians Records	1830–1904		
Guardians Bonds	1871–1919		
Probate of Wills	1841–1901		

Records (cont.)

Probate of Heirship	1880–1911
Dower Records	1829–1877
Surrogates' Minutes	1830–1903
Accounts of Estates	1829–1903
Real Estate Records	1833–1907
Miscellaneous Records	1811–1828
Orders to Publish Claims	1866–1904

Published Records and Indexes

Central New York Genealogical Society. *Tree Talks*. Syracuse, N.Y., 1961–..
▮FHL ▮NEHGS ▮NYPL ▮NYSL

Wills	1830–1840
	5: 118, 169; **6**: 18, 71; **21**: 155–56; **22**: 27; **33**: 29–30, 89–90, 151–152; **35**: 29–30, 87–88; **36**: 29–30, 87–88; **37**: 29–30; **43**: 88; **44**: 27–28; **45**: 23–24; **46**: 23–24; **47**: 23–24; **48**: 23–26
Intestate Admin.	1813–1829, 1845–1854
	37: 87–88; **38**: 29–30, 89–90; **39**: 27–28, 87–88; **40**: 27–28, 87–88; **41**: 27–28, 89–90; **42**: 27–28, 87–88; **43**: 27–28, 87–88
Estate Inventories	1811–1857
	29: 29–30, 89–90; **30**: 29–30; **31**: 29–30, 87–88, 151–60; **32**: 29–30; 89–90, 151–52; **33**: 29

Records on the Internet

New England Historic Genealogical Society

www.AmericanAncestors.org

Abstracts of Wills, Administrations and Guardianships in NY State, 1787–1835 [database].

Sampubco

www.Sampubco.com

Chautauqua County from 1830 to 1900 are indexed.

US Genweb Archives Project

www.usgwarchives.org

Includes the Sampubco indexes as well as abstracts of Intestate Records, Letters of Administration, Letters Testamentary, Court Contests, and Estate Appraisals.

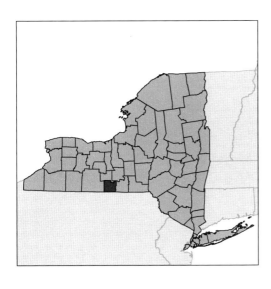

Chemung County

Chemung County Surrogate's Court

224 Lake Street
PO Box 588
Elmira, NY 14901

Date Formed	29 March 1836
County Seat	Elmira
Parent County	Tioga

Phone   (607) 737–2873
Fax   (607) 737–2874
email   None
Hours   M–F 9:00 am to 5:00 pm (building opens at 8:30)
Website   www.nycourts.gov/courts/6jd/chemung/surrogate.shtml

Special Notes

Some records are stored in vault and must be retrieved by staff. Make arrangements in advance to review records at their office.

Records on Microfilm at the Family History Library

Records

Wills	1836–1923
Administrations	1869–1889
Records of Guardianships	1836–1905
Appointment of Special Guardian	1876–1905
Final settlement, guardian	1870–1927
Final settlement, executor	1870–1907
Final settlement v. 2	1858–1870
Final settlement, Administrator	1869–1889
Minutes, Orders & Decrees	1836–1903
Probate Packets	1836–1900
Miscellaneous Records (County Clerk)	1836–1906

Indexes

Surrogates	1836–1932
Estates	1933–1970

Published Records and Indexes

Barber, Gertrude A., comp. *Abstracts of Wills of Chemung County, New York, 1836–1850.* Typescript. New York [?], n.d. ●FHL ∎FHL ∎LOC

Central New York Genealogical Society. *Tree Talks.* Syracuse, N.Y., 1961–..
∎FHL ∎NEHGS ∎NYPL ∎NYSL

Wills	1836–1845
	17: 81–82, 141–2; **18**: 29–30, 91–92, 155; **31**: 31–32;
	32: 31–32; **33**: 31–32; **34**: 31–32; **35**: 31–32; **36**: 31–32;
	37: 31–32; **38**: 31–32; **39**: 29–30
Dower	1831–1849
	8: 83, 140, 199; **9**: 26, 90; **16**: 89–90, 163–4; **17**: 81
Guardianships	1831–1855
	40: 29–30; **41**: 29–30; **42**: 29–30; **43**: 29–30; **44**: 29–30;
	45: 25–26; **46**: 25–26; **47**: 25–26; **48**: 27–28; **49**: 21–22

Records on the Internet

Sampubco
www.Sampubco.com
Chemung County wills from 1836 to 1910 are indexed.

US Genweb Archives Project
www.usgwarchives.org
Includes the Sampubco indexes as well as abstracts of Intestate Records, Letters of Administration, Letters Testamentary, Court Contests, and Estate Appraisals.

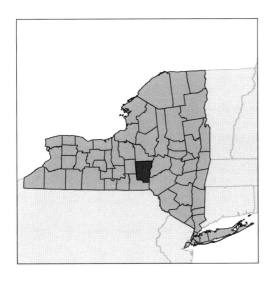

Chenango County

Chenango County Surrogate's Court

Chenango County Office Building
5 Court Street
Norwich, NY 13815

Date Formed	15 March 1798
County Seat	Norwich
Parent County	Herkimer/Tioga

Phone (607) 337–1827
Fax (607) 337–1834
email None
Hours M–F 8:30 am to 4:30 pm
Website www.nycourts.gov/courts/6jd/chenango/surrogate.shtml

Records on Microfilm at the Family History Library

Records

Wills	1792–1922
Administrators Bonds	1890–1915
Letters Testamentary & Administration	1830–1871
Letters Testamentary	1871–1904
Letters Administration	1848–1902
Letters of guardianship	1860–1921
Guardian book	1814–1878
Orders for General Guardian over 14	1878–1940
Orders for General Guardian under 14	1876–1938
Dower Book	1830,1848
Orders for Dower	1863–1868
Miscellaneous Orders, Accounts	1830–1859

Indexes

Estates	1798–1970
Wills, Proceedings	1798–1970
Index of bonds, undertakings	1878–1915

Records (cont.)

Orders & Minutes	1830–1903
Orders to prove wills	1869–1912
Orders for letters of administration	1859–1904
Orders for Publication	1884–1912
Orders for Notice to Creditors	1859–1910
Orders for sale of real estate,	1858–1901
Orders appointing appraisers,	1892–1902
Taxable transfers, taxes	1892–1907
Miscellaneous probate book	1809–1829
Final Settlement	1856–1913
Transcribed Records	1883–1894
Probate Packets	N/A

Published Records and Indexes

Barber, Gertrude A., comp. *Index to Wills of Chenango County, New York, 1797–1875.* Typescript. New York [?], 1951. ●FHL ∎NYPL ∎NYSL

Central New York Genealogical Society. *Tree Talks.* Syracuse, N.Y. 1961–.
∎FHL ∎NEHGS ∎NYPL ∎NYSL

Wills	1791–1841
	11: 197–8; **12**: 77–78; **14**: 152; **15**: 125–6, 189; **23**: 155–6; **30**: 93–4; **31**: 33–34, 89; **37**: 89–90; **38**: 33–34, 91–92; **39**: 31–32, 89–90; **46**: 27–28, 85–86; **47**: 27–28, 85–86; **48**: 29–30, 85–86; **49**: 23–24, 83–84
Letter Test.	1838–1858
	40: 89–90; **41**: 31–32, 91–92; **42**: 31–32, 89–90, 145–6; **43**: 31–32, 89–90; **44**: 31–32
Letter Test. And Administrations	
	1830–1842
	24: 157–8; **25**: 37–38, 159–60; **26**: 33–34, 93–94; **31**: 89–90; **32**: 33–34, 91–92; **33**: 33–34, 91–92; **34**: 33–34, 91–92; **35**: 33–34, 89–90; **36**: 33–34, 89–90; **37**: 33–34; **39**: 90; **40**: 31–32
Dower Records	1830–1838
	20: 154; **21**: 93–94

Curtis, Harlow D. "Early Probate Records at Norwich, N.Y." [1791–1806] *The American Genealogist.* 19 (1942): 31. ∎FHL ∎NEHGS ∎NYPL ∎NYSL

Probate Records	1791–1806

Daughters of the American Revolution, Captain John Harris Chapter, comp. "Unpublished Records–Abstracts of Wills, 1871–1900 of Chenango County." *New York DAR Genealogical Records Committee Report,* series 1, volume 318. ●FHL ∎DAR

————. "Unpublished Wills of Chenango County, New York" 3 vols. Typescript.

————. "Unpublished Wills on Record in Chenango County, New York State [liber E 1829–1848]." *New York DAR Genealogical Records Committee Report*, series 1, volume 220A.◧DAR

————. "Unpublished Wills on Record in Chenango County, New York liber F." *New York DAR Genealogical Records Committee Report,* series 1, volume 220B. ◧DAR

————. "Unpublished Wills, Norwich, Chenango County, New York State, Liber G, 1854 to 1862." *New York DAR Genealogical Records Committee Report*, series 1, volume 244. ◧DAR

New York DAR. "Unpublished Wills of Chenango County." *New York DAR Genealogical Records Committee Report*, series 1, volume 220C. ◧DAR

————. "Wills Liber C, Liber D, Chenango County, New York State." *New York DAR Genealogical Records Committee Report*, series 1, volume 220 (1957). ◧DAR

"Transcribed Records [Chenango County, New York], 1883." Typescript. ●FHL

Probate Records on the Internet

New England Historic Genealogical Society
www.AmericanAncestors.org
> Abstracts of Wills, Administrations and Guardianships in NY State, 1787–1835 [database].

New York GenWeb, Chenango County
www.usgenweb.org
> Index of Wills of Chenango County, New York from 1797–1850
> Selected Chenango County Wills (five wills abstracted out of 29 listed)

Sampubco
www.Sampubco.com
> Chenango County wills from 1792 to 1901 are indexed.

US Genweb Archives Project
www.usgwarchives.org
> Includes the Sampubco indexes as well as abstracts of Intestate Records, Letters of Administration, Letters Testamentary, Court Contests, and Estate Appraisals.

Clinton County

Clinton County Surrogate's Court

Clinton County Government Center
137 Margaret Street
Plattsburgh, NY 12901

Phone	(518) 565–4630
Fax	(518) 565–4769
email	None
Hours	M–F 9:00 am to 5:00 pm
Website	www.nycourts.gov/courts/4jd/clinton/index.shtml

Date Formed	7 March 1788
County Seat	Plattsburgh
Parent County	Washington

Records on Microfilm at the Family History Library

Records		Indexes
Wills	1807–1902	1807–1969
Administrations	1790–1908	
Guardian Records	1830–1907	1830–1969
Orders for Appointment of Guardians	1882–1890	
Dower Book	1807–1873	
Orders & Decrees	1842–1882	
Minutes of Proceedings	1856–1901	
Sale of Real Estate	1849–1886	
Miscellaneous Civil Records (County Clerk)	1885–1921	
Probate Packets	N/A	

Published Records and Indexes

Central New York Genealogical Society. *Tree Talks*. Syracuse, N.Y., 1961–.
*▮*FHL *▮*NEHGS *▮*NYPL *▮*NYSL

Wills	1807–1836
	27: 96; **28**: 35–36, 95–96; **29**: 35–36, 95–96; **31**: 35–36;
	32: 35–36; **33**: 35–36; **34**: 35–36; **35**: 35–36; **36**: 35–36;
	37: 35–36; **38**: 35–36; **39**: 33–34; **40**: 33–34; **41**: 33–34;
	42: 33–34; **43**: 33
Administrations	1790–1814
	22: 96; **23**: 93–94, 157–8; **24**: 93–94, 159; **43**: 34; **44**: 33–34;
	45: 29–30; **46**: 29–30
Guardianships	1815–1816, 1824–1837
	24: 160; **25**: 87–88, 161–2; **26**: 35–36, 95–96; **27**: 35–36,
	95–96; **47**: 29–30; **48**: 31–32; **49**: 25–26

Samuelsen, W. David. *Clinton County, New York, Will Testators Index, 1807–1902*. Salt Lake City: Sampubco, 1995. *▮*NYPL

Records on the Internet

New England Historic Genealogical Society
www.AmericanAncestors.org

Abstracts of Wills, Administrations and Guardianships in NY State, 1787–1835 [database].

Sampubco
www.Sampubco.com

Clinton County wills from 1807 to 1902 are indexed.

US Genweb Archives Project
www.usgwarchives.org

Includes the Sampubco indexes as well as abstracts of Intestate Records, Letters of Administration, Letters Testamentary, Court Contests, and Estate Appraisals.

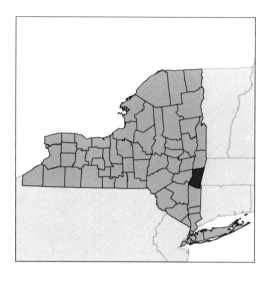

Columbia County

Columbia County Surrogate's Court

401 Union Street
Hudson, NY 12534

Phone   (518) 828–0414
Fax   (518) 828–1603
email   None
Hours   M–F 9:00 am to 5:00 pm
Website www.nycourts.gov/courts/3jd/surrogates/columbia/index.shtml

Date Formed   4 April 1786
County Seat   Hudson
Parent County   Albany

Records on Microfilm at the Family History Library

Records		Indexes	
Wills	1786–1904	Surrogates	1788–1966
Administration Bonds	1890–1903		
Administration Papers	1830–1880		
Guardian Papers	Pre–1830–1898		
Guardian Bonds	1890–1898		
Guardian Letters	1877–1898		
Will Papers	1830–1880		
Probate Packets	See Will Papers		
Decrees	1880–1901		
Letters	1830–1903		
Minutes	1831–1920		

Published Records and Indexes

Barber, Gertrude A., comp. *Abstract of Wills of Columbia County, New York, 1796–1851.* 8 vols. Typescript. New York [?], 1934–1936. ●FHL ∎LOC ∎NEHGS ∎NYPL

"Calendar of Wills of Columbia County, New York" Typescript, 1935. ∎NYSL

Central New York Genealogical Society. *Tree Talks.* Syracuse, N.Y., 1961–.
▮FHL ▮NEHGS ▮NYPL ▮NYSL

Will Papers	1830–1832
	25: 89–90; **26**: 37–38; **34**: 37–38; **35**: 37–38; **36**: 37–38;
	37: 37–38; **38**: 37
Administrations	1830
	33: 37–38; **34**: 37
Dower	1808–1821
	23: 159–60; **24**: 95–96
Guardianships	1811–1826
	39: 35–36; **40**: 35–36; **43**: 36; **46**: 31–32; **47**: 31–32, 87–88

The Columbia. Rhinebeck, N.Y.: Valley Quarterlies, 1985–1998. ▮FHL ▮NEHGS ▮NYPL

Guardianships	1802–1866
	1: 57–59, 116–120; **2**: 17–20, 39–43, 82–96, 111–15;
	3: 21–25, 55–58, 88–93, 135–38; **4**: 7–10, 57–62, 102–107,
	123–28; **5**: 23–27, 55–60, 93–98, 123–26; **6**: 17–20, 63–66,
	91–94, 133–36; **7**: 3–8, 55–60, 75–80, 131–136; **8**: 3–4

Kelly, Arthur C. M. *Will Abstracts of Columbia County, New York, 1786–1851.* 2 vols. Rhinebeck, N.Y.: Kinship, 2007. ▮FHL

Records on the Internet

New England Historic Genealogical Society
www.AmericanAncestors.org

Abstracts of Wills, Administrations and Guardianships in NY State, 1787–1835 [database].

Sampubco
www.Sampubco.com

Columbia County wills from 1786 to 1904 are indexed.

US Genweb Archives Project
www.usgwarchives.org

Includes the Sampubco indexes as well as abstracts of Intestate Records, Letters of Administration, Letters Testamentary, Court Contests, and Estate Appraisals.

Cortland County

Cortland County Surrogate's Court

Cortland County Courthouse
46 Greenbush Street, Suite 301
Cortland, NY 13045–2725

Phone	(607) 753–5355
Fax	(607) 756–3409
email	None
Hours	M–F 9:00 am to 5:00 pm
	8:30 am to 4:30 pm (summer)
Website	www.nycourts.gov/courts/6jd/cortland/surrogate.shtml

Date Formed	8 April 1808
County Seat	Cortland
Parent County	Onondaga

Special Notes

Indexes of court files are available at the surrogate's court. Wills are available in hard copy or on microfilm. Some records are stored off–site. They can be ordered through correspondence or reviewed at the office with a prior written request that includes the file number.

Records on Microfilm at the Family History Library

Records

Wills, Administrations	1809–1832
Wills	1832–1908
Administrations	1832–1914
Guardianships	1832–1935
Estate Files	1810–1893
Minutes, orders, wills,	1889–1910
Minutes, orders, Administration	1887–1907
Minutes and Entries	
Minutes, Orders, Decrees	1832–1887
Orders, citations	1881–1908

Indexes

Wills, Admins.	1808–1970
Surrogates	1927–1970

Records (cont.)		Indexes (cont.)	
Miscellaneous Records,			
County Clerk	1830–1919	Index	1830–1960
Probate packets	See Estate Files		

Published Records and Indexes

Central New York Genealogical Society. *Tree Talks.* Syracuse, N.Y., 1961–.
*▮*FHL *▮*NEHGS *▮*NYPL *▮*NYSL

Wills & Admin.	1809–1824, 1825–1846
	7: 83, 136, 191; **9**: 94, 157; **11**: 33–34, 81–82, 153–4; **12**: 148, 199–00; **13**: 27–28, 80; **17**: 145–146; **18**: 33–34, 95–96, 159; **19**: 161–2; **20**: 35–36, 97–98, 155–60; **23**: 34; **24**: 97–98; **25**: 164; **26**: 39–40, 97–98, 149–50; **27**: 39–40, 97–98, 149–50; **28**: 37–38, 97–98, 151–2; **29**: 37–38, 97–98; **38**: 149–150; **39**: 37–38, 91–92, 147–8; **40**: 37–38, 91–92, 147–8; **41**: 37–38, 93–94, 147–8; **42**: 37–38, 91; **45**: 145–6; **46**: 33–34, 87–88, 145–6; **47**: 33–34, 89–90, 145–6; **48**: 33–34, 87–88, 145–6; **49**: 27–30, 85–86, 145–6
Letters Test. And Admin	1832–1857
	29: 153–4; **30**: 35–36, 95–96, 157–8; **31**: 37–38, 91–92, 153–4; **32**: 39–40, 93–94, 153–4; **33**: 39–40, 93–94, 153–4; **34**: 39–40, 93–94, 149–50
Guardianship	1832–1859
	34: 150; **35**: 39–40, 91–92, 149–50; **36**: 39–40, 91–92, 149–50; **37**: 39–40, 91–92, 151–2; **38**: 39–40; **43**: 147–8; **44**: 37–38, 91–92, 147–148; **45**: 33–34, 87–88, 145

Samuelsen, W. David. "Cortland County, New York, Will Testators Index, 1832–1909." Salt Lake City: Sampubco, 1996. **●**FHL

Records on the Internet

New England Historic Genealogical Society
www.AmericanAncestors.org
Abstracts of Wills, Administrations and Guardianships in NY State, 1787–1835 [database].

Sampubco
www.Sampubco.com
Cortland County wills from 1832 to 1908 are indexed.

US Genweb Archives Project
www.usgwarchives.org
Includes the Sampubco indexes as well as abstracts of Intestate Records, Letters of Administration, Letters Testamentary, Court Contests, and Estate Appraisals.

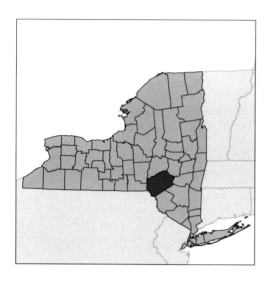

Delaware County

Delaware County Surrogate's Court

Delaware County Courthouse
3 Court Street
Delhi, NY 13753

Date Formed	10 March 1797
County Seat	Delhi
Parent Counties	Otsego, Ulster

Phone   (607) 746–2126
Fax   (607) 746–3253
email   None
Hours   M–F 9:00 am to 5:00 pm (closed for lunch)
Website www.nycourts.gov/courts/6jd/delaware/surrogate.shtml

Special Notes

Some wills at the Delaware County Surrogate's Court have been scanned. Because they are in special software installed at the court, they are only available for research and copying at the courthouse. Anyone interested in getting a copy of a will should contact the clerk of the surrogate court at the above address (please include a SASE).

Records on Microfilm at the Family History Library

Records		Indexes	
Wills	1797–1926	Wills	1797–1963
Administrations	1822–1930	Guardians	1797–1965
Letters of Administration and Testamentary,	1830–1930		
Letters of Guardianship & Guardian Records	1803–1885		
Record of Guardians	1864–1880		
Guardian Decrees & Letters of guardianship	1881–1899		

Records (cont.)

Estate Papers and Proceedings	1797–1900
Minutes	1835–1897
Accounts of executors,	
& administration	1832–1904
Bonds	1890–1916
Sales of Real Estate	1832–1910
Probate Packets	See Estate Papers and Proceedings (Probate packets from 1900–1915 catalogued under Wills)

Published Records and Indexes

Barber, Gertrude A., comp. *Abstracts of Wills of Delaware County, New York, 1796–1875.* 6 vols. in 1. Typescript. New York [?], n.d. ⬤FHL ◤LOC ◤NEHGS ◤NYPL

———. *Index of Wills, Delaware County, New York, from 1797–1885.* Typescript. New York [?], n.d. ⬤FHL ◤NYPL

———. *Letters of Administration of Delaware County, New York, [1797–1875].* 4 vols. in 1. Typescript. New York [?], 1939. ⬤FHL ◤LOC ◤NEHGS ◤NYPL

Central New York Genealogical Society. *Tree Talks.* Syracuse, N.Y., 1961–. ◤FHL ◤NEHGS ◤NYPL ◤NYSL

Wills	1797
	41: 40; **42**: 39–40; **43**: 39–40; **44**: 39–40; **45**: 35–36; **46**: 35–36; **47**: 35–36; **48**: 35–36
Guardians Index:	1833–1885
Guardianships	1832–1848, 1858
	3: 118; **4**: 27, 78, 133, 188; **6**: 22; **29**: 40, 99–100; **30**: 37–38, 97–98, 159–60; **31**: 39–40
Dower:	1833–1877
	10: 96, 159; **12**: 31; **24**: 99–100; **28**: 39

Cowen, Minnie. "Index of Wills, Delaware County, New York, 1795–1885." Typescript, 1934.

"Delhi, NY Probates" [1836–1875] *Rota-Gene.* 11 (1990): 20. Sarasota, Fla.: International Genealogy Fellowship of Rotarians, 1980–. ◤FHL ◤NEHGS

Witherbee, Mary Kales. "Miscellaneous Records of Delaware County, New York." *New York DAR Genealogical Records Committee Report*, series 1, volume 530 (1982). ◤DAR

Records on the Internet

Delaware County, NY Genealogy and History Site

www.dcnyhistory.org:

> Ogborn, Linda, abst. "Early Wills of Delaware County, NY Abstracted from Gertrude Barber's Records" (posted April 23, 2009).
>
> Goodrich, Victor B., comp. "Index to Delaware County, New York Probate Files for Persons Dying 1900 or Earlier" (posted by Linda Ogborn, March 5, 2001).

New England Historic Genealogical Society

www.AmericanAncestors.org

> Abstracts of Wills, Administrations and Guardianships in NY State, 1787–1835 [database].

Sampubco

www.Sampubco.com

> Delaware County wills from 1797 to 1916 are indexed.

US Genweb Archives Project

www.usgwarchives.org

> Includes the Sampubco indexes as well as abstracts of Intestate Records, Letters of Administration, Letters Testamentary, Court Contests, and Estate Appraisals.

Dutchess County

Dutchess County Surrogate's Court

10 Market Street
Poughkeepsie, NY 12601

Phone	(845) 486–2235
Fax	(845) 486–2234
email	None
Hours	M–F 9:00 am to 5:00 pm
Website	www.nycourts.gov/courts/9jd/dutchess/index.shtml

Date Formed	1 November 1683
County Seat	Poughkeepsie
Parent County	Original

Records on Microfilm at the Family History Library

Records		Indexes	
Wills	1751–1903	Surrogates	1751–1934
Wills (Court of Common Pleas)	1790–1828		
Administrations	1787–1865		
Letters of Administration (extracts)	1788–1800		
Letters Testamentary and of Administration	1787–1865		
Dower Records	1800–1852		
Real Estate Record	1821–1853		
Surrogates Minutes	1830–1866		
Probate Packets	1793–1868		

Published Records and Indexes

Adriance Memorial Library. "Index to Wills, 1721–1906 [selected], Wills, 1799–1956 [includes holographic wills], Index to Letters [selected]." ●FHL ⍁LOC

Barber, Gertrude A., comp. "Abstracts of Wills of Dutchess County, New York, Oct. 1834–Oct. 1839." Typescript. [New York?], 1944. ●FHL

———. "Index to Wills of Dutchess County, New York, 1812–1832." Typescript. n.d. ▮LOC ▮NYPL

Cowen, Minnie, abst. *Abstracts of Wills of Dutchess County, New York, 1752–1834.* 12 vols. Typescript, 1941. ●FHL ▮LOC ▮NYPL

Dutchess County Genealogical Society. *The Dutchess.* Poughkeepsie, N.Y., 1973–. ▮FHL ▮NEHGS ▮NYPL ▮NYSL

Wills	1798–1839
	4: (No.3) 32–34, (No. 4) 3–8; **5**: (No. 1) 30–33, (No. 2) 3–6, (No. 4)32–33; **6**: (No. 1) 13–18, (No. 2) 25–32, (No. 3) 5–10, (No. 4) 30–32; **7**: (No. 1) 17–20, (No. 2) 27–31, (No. 3) 26–34, (No. 4) 19–26; **8**: (No. 1) 8–15, (No. 2) 18–24, (No. 3) 21–29, (No. 4) 12–17; **9**: (No. 1) 3–8, (No. 2) 3–7, (No. 3) 26–30, (No. 4) 31–33; **10**: (No. 1) 16–24, (No. 2) 3–5; (No. 3) 20–23, (No. 4) 28–33; **11**: (No. 1) 18–25, (No. 2) 56–61, (No. 3) 83–89, (No. 4) 111–15; **12**: 20–24, 55–61, 83–91, 111–17; **13**: 3–11, 54–60, 75–82, 137–44; **14**: 23–26, 47–54, 85–89, 116–21; **15**: 5–11, 61–66, 79–84, 117–22; **16**: 18–22, 39–45, 91–94, 127–32; **17**: 9–14, 50–54, 81–84, 131–34; **18**: 3–6, 47–51, 95–98, 137–42; **19**: 13–18, 55–60, 103–106, 129–32; **20**: 25–28, 45–52, 101–105, 131–36; **21**: 19–22, 39–44
Will Index	18th Century
	21: 141–42; **22**: 34
	1787–1797 (index to *NYGB Record* article below)
	4: (No. 2) 12–16
	1837–1905
	24: 75–80, 137–143; **25**: 7–14, 59–66; 79–86; 115–24; **26**: 3–12, 49–56, 103–107, 128–33; **27**: 1–8, 61–70, 82–91, 129–136; **28**: 5–14, 57–64, 78–89, 123–30; **29**: 3–10, 61–68, 98

Kelly, Arthur C. M. *Dutchess County, New York, Probate Records, 1787–1865: Register of Wills and Letters Testamentary and of Administrations in the Surrogate's Office, Poughkeepsie, New York.* Rhinebeck, N.Y.: Kinship, 1997. ▮FHL ▮NEHGS

New York Genealogical and Biographical Society. *New York Genealogical and Biographical Record.* New York, 1870–. ▮FHL ▮NEHGS

Wills	1787–1797
	61: 6–13, 119–126, 257–263, 381–386; **62**: 58–59

Records on the Internet

Dutchess County, New York GenWeb

www.usgenweb.com

Selected abstracts of Dutchess County wills (these appear to be different than the abstracts in the US Genweb Archives Project).

New England Historic Genealogical Society

www.AmericanAncestors.org

Abstracts of Wills, Administrations and Guardianships in NY State, 1787–1835 [database]. Some pre-1787 wills appear for Dutchess County.

Sampubco

www.Sampubco.com

Dutchess County wills are indexed 1797 to 1916.

US Genweb Archives Project

www.usgwarchives.org

Includes the Sampubco indexes as well as abstracts of Intestate Records, Letters of Administration, Letters Testamentary, Court Contests, and Estate Appraisals.

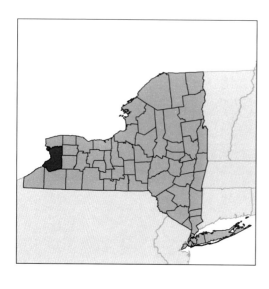

Erie County

Erie County Surrogate's Court

Erie County Hall
92 Franklin Street
Buffalo, NY 14202

Phone	(716) 845–2560
Fax	(716) 853–3741

Date Formed	2 April 1821
County Seat	Buffalo
Parent County	Niagara

Record Room

Phone	(716) 845–2585
email	mmartoch@courts.state.ny.us
Hours	M–F 9:00 am to 5:00 pm
Website	www.nycourthelp.gov/eriesurrct1.htm
	www.nycourts.gov/courts/8jd/Erie/surrogates/index.shtml

Records on Microfilm at the Family History Library

Records		Indexes	
Wills	No registered wills on film after 1832	Estates	1800–1929
Wills, Letters Testamentary, Administration, Guardianship	1819–1832		
Letters of administration	1826–1901		
Letters testamentary	1832–1900		
Surrogate Records	1800–1905		
Miscellaneous Records County Clerk	1808–1907		
Probate Packets	See Surrogate Records		

Published Records and Indexes

Central New York Genealogical Society. *Tree Talks*. Syracuse, N.Y., 1961–.
∎FHL ∎NEHGS ∎NYPL ∎NYSL

Wills, Letters Test, Admin, Guardianship
 1821–1832
 32: 43–44; **33**: 43–44; **34**: 43–44; **35**: 43–44; **36**: 43–44;
 37: 43–44; **38**: 43–44; **41**: 41–42; **42**: 41–42; **43**: 41–42;
 44: 41–42; **45**: 37–38

Guardianship 1840–1845
 48: 38–40

Administrations 1819–1832
 45: 38; **46**: 37–38; **47**: 37–38; **48**: 37

Western New York Genealogical Society. *Western New York Genealogical Society Journal.*
 Hamburg, N.Y., 1974–. ∎FHL ∎NEHGS ∎NYPL ∎NYSL

Surrogate's Index To 1860
 24: 54–64, 117–25; **25**: 11–17, 73–81, 115–122, 172–76; **26**:
 61–67, 106–113, 165–70
 1861–1880
 32: 112–30, 150–65; **33**: 6–21, 55–68, 105–123, 152–65; **34**:
 13–21, 59–76, 109–121, 161–73
 1811–1900 [in progress]
 35: 115–32, 172–79; **36**: 20–34, 63–75, 106–122, 160–68;
 37: 12–22

Niagara County Genealogical Society Newsletter. Lockport, N.Y.: Niagara County
 Genealogical Society, 1979––.

Wills and Probate 1800–1840
 7: (No. 3), (No. 4); **8**: (No. 2); **9**: (No. 1) 9–10, (No. 2) 9–10

Records on the Internet

New England Historic Genealogical Society

www.AmericanAncestors.org
 Abstracts of Wills, Administrations and Guardianships in NY State, 1787–1835
 [database].

US Genweb Archives Project

www.usgwarchives.org
 Includes the Sampubco indexes as well as abstracts of Intestate Records, Letters of
 Administration, Letters Testamentary, Court Contests, and Estate Appraisals.

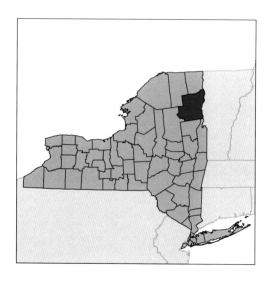

Essex County

Essex County Surrogate's Office
7559 Court Street
P.O. Box 217
Elizabethtown, NY 12932

Phone	(518) 873–3384
Fax	(518) 873–3731
Email	None
Hours	M–F 9:00 am to 5:00 pm
Website	www.nycourts.gov/courts/4jd/essex/index.shtml

Date Formed	1 March 1799
County Seat	Elizabethtown
Parent County	Clinton

Special Notes

Some older probate records are filed among miscellaneous loose papers, arranged somewhat alphabetically, in the County Clerk's Office.

Records on Microfilm at the Family History Library

Records		Indexes	
Wills	1803–1904	Surrogates	1799–1938
Letters	1831–1902		
Guardianship Records	1847–1901		
Guardianship Records	1869–1910		
Probate Packets	N/A		

Published Records and Indexes

Central New York Genealogical Society. *Tree Talks*. Syracuse, N.Y., 1961–.
IFHL **I**NEHGS **I**NYPL **I**NYSL

Wills and Admin.   1803–1816
22: 99–100; **23**: 161–2; **24**: 101; **39**: 43–44; **41**: 43–44;
42: 43–44; **43**: 43–44; **44**: 43–44; **45**: 39–40; **46**: 39–40;
47: 39–40; **48**: 41–42; **49**: 33–34

Administrations   1811
Dower   1830–1842
29: 41–42; **30**: 39–40

Samuelsen, W. David. *Essex County, New York, Will Testators Index, 1803–1904*. Salt Lake City: Sampubco, 1996. **⊙**FHL

Witherbee, Mary Kales. "Unpublished Records, Essex County." *New York DAR Genealogical Records Committee Report*, series 1, volume 220 (1966). **I**DAR

Records on the Internet

New England Historic Genealogical Society
www.AmericanAncestors.org
Abstracts of Wills, Administrations and Guardianships in NY State, 1787–1835 [database].

Sampubco
www.Sampubco.com
Essex County wills from 1803 to 1904 are indexed.

US Genweb Archives Project
www.usgwarchives.org
Includes the Sampubco indexes as well as abstracts of Intestate Records, Letters of Administration, Letters Testamentary, Court Contests, and Estate Appraisals.

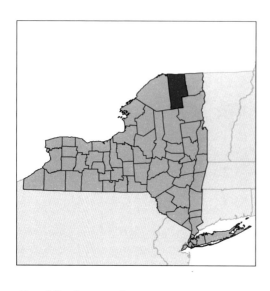

Franklin County

Franklin County Surrogate's Court

Franklin County Courthouse
355 West Main Street #3223
Malone, NY 12953–1817

Phone	(518) 481–1736
Fax	(518) 481–1443
email	None
Hours	M–F 9:00 am to 5:00 pm (Sep–May)
	M–F 8:00 am to 4:00 pm (Jun–Aug)
Website	www.nycourts.gov/courts/4jd/franklin/surrogates.shtml

Date Formed	11 March 1808
County Seat	Malone
Parent County	Clinton, Montgomery, and Essex

Records on Microfilm at the Family History Library

Records		Indexes
Wills	1809–1919	1809–1900
Probate of Wills	1894–1920	
Decrees Admitting Wills to Probate	1879–1916	
Wills Recopied from Faded Pages	1809–1870	
Letters Testamentary and Administration	1847–1919	
Bonds, administrators	1890–1920	
Letters of guardianship	1842–1913	
Special guardian order	1908–1930	
Admeasurement of Dower	1839–1880	
Orders and decrees	1847–1879	
Daybook (proceedings of court)	1880–1902	
Decrees in administration	1868–1909	
Miscellaneous orders (court records)	1892–1910	

Records (cont.)

Sale of real estate	1839–1927
Final decrees	1878–1912
Probate Packets	N/A

Published Records and Indexes

Central New York Genealogical Society. *Tree Talks.* Syracuse, N.Y., 1961–.
∥FHL **∥**NEHGS **∥**NYPL **∥**NYSL

Wills, Administration	1809–1847
	9: 33, 97; **22**: 102; **23**: 39–40; **24**: 37–38; **25**: 97–98;
	26: 47–48; **27**: 47–48; **28**: 43–44
Administrations	1809–1826
Dower	1839–1850
	18: 163–4; **20**: 101
Guardianships	1842–1864
	38: 48; **39**: 45–46; **40**: 45–46; **41**: 45–46; **42**: 45–46
Surrogates Records	1832–1837
	8: 147, 206; **36**: 47–48; **37**: 47–48; **38**: 47–48; **43**: 45–46;
	45: 42

Samuelsen, W. David. *Franklin County, New York, Will Testators Index, 1809–1919.* Salt Lake City: Sampubco, 1994. **∥**FHL **∥**NYPL

Records on the Internet

New England Historic Genealogical Society
www.AmericanAncestors.org
Abstracts of Wills, Administrations and Guardianships in NY State, 1787–1835 [database].

Sampubco
www.Sampubco.com
Franklin County wills from 1809 to 1919 are indexed.

US Genweb Archives Project
www.usgwarchives.org
Includes the Sampubco indexes as well as abstracts of Intestate Records, Letters of Administration, Letters Testamentary, Court Contests, and Estate Appraisals.

Fulton County

Fulton County Surrogate's Court

223 West Main Street
Johnstown, NY 12095

Phone	(518) 736–5685
Fax	(518) 762–6372
email	None
Hours	M–F 8:00 am to 5:00 pm (Sep–Jun)
	M–F 8:00 am to 4:00 pm (Jul–Labor Day)
	May be closed during lunch hours.
Website	www.nycourts.gov/courts/4jd/fulton/index.shtml

Date Formed	18 April 1838
County Seat	Johnstown
Parent County	Montgomery

Records on Microfilm at the Family History Library

Records

Wills	1789–1937
Letters testamentary	1789–1901
Orders, prob. of wills	1877–1908
Letters Administrations	1894–1907
Orders, appointing admins.	1877–1903
Administrators bonds	1899–1904
Guardians bonds & appt.	1877–1906
Letters of guardianship	1838–1907
Dower Records	1818–1861
Minutes	1838–1903
General orders	1877–1910
Orders, final settlement	1879–1901
Sales of real estate	1838–1885
Orders, publ. of citation	1897–1927
Orders, coll. inheritance tax	1893–1906
Probate Packets	N/A

Indexes

Surrogates	1830–1967

Published Records and Indexes

Central New York Genealogical Society. *Tree Talks*. Syracuse, N.Y., 1961–.
*FHL *NEHGS *NYPL *NYSL

Wills	1838–1846
	12: 155–6; **13**: 34; **25**: 166; **26**: 49–60; **27**: 49–50; **28**: 45–46;
	29: 45–46; **30**: 43–44; **31**: 43–44, 97–98; **32**: 47–48;
	33: 49–50; **34**: 49–50; **35**: 49–50; **36**: 49–50; **37**: 49–50;
	38: 49–50; **39**: 47–48; **40**: 47–48; **41**: 47–48; **42**: 47–48;
	43: 47–48; **44**: 47–48
Dower:	1838–1839
	12: 156; **13**: 33

Samuelsen, W. David. *Fulton County, New York Will Testators Index, 1789–1937*. Salt Lake City: Sampubco, 1996. ●FHL

Records on the Internet

Sampubco
www.Sampubco.com
Fulton County wills from 1789 to 1937 are indexed.

US Genweb Archives Project
www.usgwarchives.org
Includes the Sampubco indexes as well as abstracts of Intestate Records, Letters of Administration, Letters Testamentary, Court Contests, and Estate Appraisals.

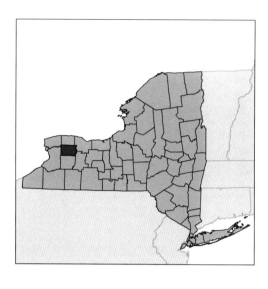

Genesee County

Genesee County Surrogate's Court

Courts Facility Building
1 West Main Street
Batavia, NY 14020

Date Formed	30 March 1802
County Seat	Batavia
Parent County	Ontario

Phone   (585) 344–2550, Ext. 2237
Fax   (585) 344–8517
email   None
Hours   M–F 9:00 am to 5:00 pm
Website   www.nycourts.gov/courts/8jd/Genesee/surrogates.shtml

Special Notes

Probate petitions are in probate books (also available on film).

Records on Microfilm at the Family History Library

Records		Indexes	
Wills	1809–1911	Surrogates	1805–1939
Letters Testamentary	1856–1901		
Letters of testamentary, & administration	1830–1854		
Administrations	1856–1907		
Letters of administration	1805–1856, 1872–1901		
Letters of guardianship	1810–1906		
Special guardians	1856–1909		
Probate books	1856–1908		
Bonds	1890–1901		
Orders	1809–1901		
Orders to Advertise	1856–1904		

Records (cont.)

Appraisers	1856–1902
Land sales	1868–1911
Miscellaneous records	1897–1909
Decrees	1856–1901
Probate Packets	N/A

Published Records and Indexes

Central New York Genealogical Society. *Tree Talks*. Syracuse, N.Y., 1961–.
    ∥FHL ∥NEHGS ∥NYPL ∥NYSL

Wills	1813–1830
	4: 31, 82, 137, 193; **5**: 72, 126, 176; **6**: 26, 79, 122; **7**: 33, 88, 141, 196; **8**: 91, 149; **11**: 159–60; **12**: 38, 157; **26**: 52; **27**: 51–52; **28**: 47; **46**: 45–46; **47**: 45–46; **48**: 47–48; **49**: 39–40
Letters Test. And Admin	1830–1838
	28: 47–48; **29**: 47–48; **30**: 45–46; **31**: 45–46; **32**: 49–50, 97–98; **33**: 51–52; **34**: 51–52; **35**: 51–52
Administrations	1813–1821
	35: 52; **36**: 51–52; **37**: 51–52; **38**: 51–52; **39**: 49–50; **40**: 49–50; **41**: 49–50; **42**: 49–50; **43**: 49–50; **44**: 49–50; **45**: 45–46

Haynes, Myrte Rice. "Settlements of Estates of Early Residents in Monroe County, New York," in Janet Wethy Foley, *Early Settlers of New York State, 1934–1942*. 2 vols. Reprint, Baltimore: Genealogical Publishing Co., 1993. Vol. 2, pp. 361, 377, 393, 409, 425, 441, 458, 473, 489. [Estates of Monroe County residents in Genesee and Ontario Counties before Monroe was created in 1821] ∥FHL ∥NEHGS

Records on the Internet

New England Historic Genealogical Society
www.AmericanAncestors.org
    Abstracts of Wills, Administrations and Guardianships in NY State, 1787–1835 [database].

Sampubco
www.Sampubco.com
    Genesee County wills from 1809 to 1901 are indexed.

US Genweb Archives Project
www.usgwarchives.org
    Includes the Sampubco indexes as well as abstracts of Intestate Records, Letters of Administration, Letters Testamentary, Court Contests, and Estate Appraisals.

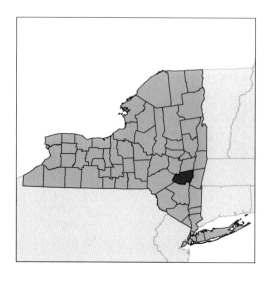

Greene County

Greene County Surrogate's Court

Greene County Courthouse
320 Main Street
Catskill, NY 12414

Date Formed	25 March 1800
County Seat	Catskill
Parent County	Albany and Ulster

Phone   (518) 444–8750
Fax   (518) 943–5811
email   None
Hours   M–F 9:00 am to 5:00 pm (hours may be shorter in Summer)
Website www.nycourts.gov/courts/3jd/surrogates/greene/index.shtml

Greene County Historical Society

Vedder Research Library
US Route 9W
Coxsackie, NY 12051

Mailing Address

PO Box 44
Coxsackie, NY 12051–044

Phone   (518) 731–1033
Fax   None
Email   gchsvl@mhcable.com
Hours   T–W 10:00 am to 4:00 pm, Sat 9
Website www.gchistory.org

Special Notes

Records prior to 1920 are available on microfilm at the Surrogate's Court. Original records for that period are at the Greene County Historical Society.

Records on Microfilm at the Family History Library

Records		Indexes	
Wills	1800–1923	Surrogates	1800–1930
Letters Testamentary	1830–1917		
Administrations	1804–1903		
Letters Administration	1804–1900		
Administration Bonds	1890–1901		
Executors & Administrators Records	1831–1902		
Guardianships	1816–1912		
Estate Papers	Pre–1800 to Post–1883 (alphabetized by first letter of surname)		
Minutebook	1830–1899		
Probate Packets	See Estate Papers		

Published Records and Indexes

Barber, Gertrude A. *Index of Wills, Greene County, New York, 1803–1875.* Rochester, N.Y.: n.p., 1973. ●FHL ▮NYPL

Central New York Genealogical Society. *Tree Talks.* Syracuse, N.Y., 1961–. ▮FHL ▮NEHGS ▮NYPL ▮NYSL

Wills	1803–1808, 1806–1813
	32: 51–52, 99–100; **33**: 53–54; **34**: 53–54; **35**: 53–54; **36**: 53;
	37: 53–54; **38**: 53
Administrations	1804–1831
	23: 164–6; **24**: 165–6; **25**: 167–8; **26**: 53–54; **38**: 54;
	39: 51–52; **40**: 51–52; **41**: 51–52; **42**: 51–52; **43**: 51–52;
	44: 51–52; **45**: 47–48
Guardianships	1841–1845
	45: 48; **46**: 47–48; **47**: 47–48, 91–92

Greene Genes: A Genealogical Quarterly About Greene County, New York. Maplecrest, N.Y.: Patricia Morrow, 1988–1999. ▮FHL ▮NEHGS ▮NYPL ▮NYSL

Wills	1803–1808
	1: 58–70
	1882–1884
	5: 79–112
	1902–1905
	3: 89–122, 131–54
Letters of Admin.	1840–1848
	2: 105–114

Sawyer, Ray C., comp. *Abstracts of Wills of Greene County, New York, 1800–1900.* 3 vols. Typescript, 1933–1934. ●FHL ▮LOC ▮NEHGS ▮NYPL ▮NYSL

Records on the Internet

New England Historic Genealogical Society
www.AmericanAncestors.org

Abstracts of Wills, Administrations and Guardianships in NY State, 1787–1835 [database].

Sampubco
www.Sampubco.com

Greene County wills from 1800 to 1923 are indexed.

US Genweb Archives Project
www.usgwarchives.org

Includes the Sampubco indexes as well as abstracts of Intestate Records, Letters of Administration, Letters Testamentary, Court Contests, and Estate Appraisals.

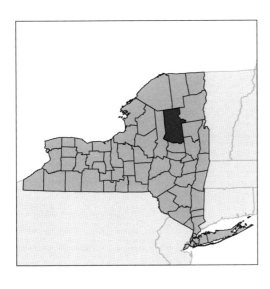

Hamilton County

Hamilton County Surrogate's Court

79 White Birch Lane
PO Box 780
Indian Lake, NY 12842

Phone	(518) 648–5411
Fax	(518) 648–6286
email	None
Hours	M–F 8:30 am to 4:30 pm
Website	www.nycourts.gov/courts/4jd/hamilton/index.shtml

Date Formed	12 April 1816
County Seat	Lake Pleasant
Parent County	Montgomery

Records on Microfilm at the Family History Library

Records	Indexes
Wills	1861–1934
Letters Testamentary, Administration, & Guardianship	1878–1920
Book of Minutes	1878–1921
Records of Settlements	1906–1920
Estate Papers	1861–1908
Probate Packets	See Estate Papers

Published Records and Indexes

Central New York Genealogical Society. *Tree Talks*. Syracuse, N.Y., 1961–.

▮FHL **▮**NEHGS **▮**NYPL **▮**NYSL

Wills	1858–1893
	20: 105–6, 165–6; **21**: 105–6

Letters Test, Administrations, Guardianship
                      1858–1917
                      22: 107; **23**: 103
Guardianships   1864–1917

Records on the Internet

Sampubco

www.Sampubco.com

    Hamilton County wills from 1878 to 1934 are indexed.

US Genweb Archives Project

www.usgwarchives.org

    Includes the Sampubco indexes as well as abstracts of Intestate Records, Letters of Administration, Letters Testamentary, Court Contests, and Estate Appraisals.

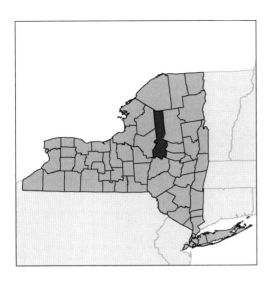

Herkimer County

Herkimer County Surrogate's Court

Herkimer County
Office & Court Facility
301 North Washington St. #5550
Herkimer, NY 13350

Phone	(315) 867–1367
Fax	(315) 866–1722
email	None
Hours	M–F 8:30 am to 4:30 pm (Sep–May)
	M–F 8:30 am to 4:00 pm (Jun–Aug)
Website	www.nycourts.gov/courts/5jd/herkimer/index.shtml

Date Formed	16 February 1791
County Seat	Herkimer
Parent County	Montgomery

Records on Microfilm at the Family History Library

Records		Indexes	
Wills	1792–1917	Wills	1792–1970
Letters Testamentary	1861–1902		
Letters Administration	1792–1970	Administration	1792–1870
Bonds (Administration)	1890–1899		
Guardianship Records	1800–1920	Guardians	1800–1969
Guardian Bonds	1890–1906		
Surrogate's records	1821–1869		
Decrees on Final Accounts	1800–1902		
Minutes, Orders, and Decrees (Wills)	1870–1909		
Minutes, Orders, and Decrees (Administration)	1868–1911		
Estate Papers	1792–1900		
(alphabetized by first letter of surname)			

Records (cont.)

Miscellaneous Records	
(County Clerk)	1882–1901
Probate Packets	See Estate Papers

Published Records and Indexes

Ancestral Notes from Chedwato. West Hartford, Conn.: Chedwato Service, 1954–1968.
ⅡFHL ⅡNEHGS ⅡNYPL ⅡNYSL

Guardianships	1803–1818

Central New York Genealogical Society. *Tree Talks.* Syracuse, N.Y., 1961–.
ⅡFHL ⅡNEHGS ⅡNYPL ⅡNYSL

Wills	1792–1819
	4: 139, 195; **7**: 34, 89, 142, 197; **8**: 31, 91, 150, 209; **9**: 36, 99, 163, 226; **10**: 40, 102, 166, 235; **25**: 41–42; **26**: 99; **30**: 99–100; **31**: 47–48, 99–100; **32**: 53–54, 101–02; **33**: 97; **37**: 55–56, 93–94; **46**: 90; **47**: 49–50, 93–94; **48**: 49–50, 89–90; **49**: 41–42, 89–90
Administrations	1792–1821
	29: 101–02; **30**: 47–48; **44**: 54, 93–94; **45**: 49–50, 89–90; **46**: 49–50, 89–90
Guardianships	1800–1820
	38: 55–56, 95–96; **39**: 53–54, 93–94; **40**: 53–54, 93–94; **41**: 53–54, 95–96; **42**: 53–54, 93–94; **43**: 53–54, 93–94; **44**: 53

Samuelsen, W. David. *Herkimer County, New York Will Testators Index, 1792–1921.* Salt Lake City: Sampubco, 1996. ●FHL

The Searcher: A Publication of the Southern California Genealogical Society. Burbank, Calif.: Southern California Genealogical Society, 1963–. **ⅡFHL ⅡNEHGS ⅡNYPL ⅡNYSL**

Surrogates Records	1830
	5: 185

Records on the Internet

New England Historic Genealogical Society
www.AmericanAncestors.org
Abstracts of Wills, Administrations and Guardianships in NY State, 1787–1835 [database].

New York GenWeb, Herkimer County
www.usgenweb.org
Herkimer/Montgomery Counties Wills and Deeds Bulletin Boards — voluntary contributions of will abstracts.

Sampubco

www.Sampubco.com

Herkimer County wills for 1792 to 1917 are indexed.

US Genweb Archives Project

www.usgwarchives.org

Includes the Sampubco indexes as well as abstracts of Intestate Records, Letters of Administration, Letters Testamentary, Court Contests, and Estate Appraisals.

Jefferson County

Jefferson County Surrogate's Court

Jefferson County Court Complex
County Office Building
163 Arsenal Street
Watertown, NY 13601

Date Formed	28 March 1805
County Seat	Watertown
Parent County	Oneida

Phone   (315) 785–3019
Fax   (315) 785–5194
email   None
Hours   M–F 8:30 am to 4:30 pm (Labor Day–May)
             M–F 8:30 am to 4:00 pm (Jun to Labor Day)
Website   www.nycourts.gov/courts/5jd/jefferson/index.shtml

Records on Microfilm at the Family History Library

Records		Indexes
Wills	1830–1913	1830–1900
Letters Testamentary	1850–1900	
Letters Administration	1830–1924	1830–1900
Guardianship Bonds	1890–1906	
Letters of Guardianship	1851–1908	
Estate Papers	1805–1945	
Minutes, Orders & Decrees	1830–1910	1830–1900
Disposal of real estate	1832–1895	
Probate Packets	See Estate Papers	

Published Records and Indexes

Central New York Genealogical Society. *Tree Talks*. Syracuse, N.Y., 1961–.
  ⫮FHL ⫮NEHGS ⫮NYPL ⫮NYSL

Wills	1830–1835
	28: 52, 103–4; **29**: 51–52, 103–4; **40**: 96, 149–50; **41**: 97–98, 149–50; **42**: 95–96, 149–50; **43**: 95–96, 149–50; **44**: 95–96, 149–50; **45**: 91
Guardianship	1831–1842
	26: 153–4; **27**: 101; **30**: 49–50, 101–2; **31**: 49–50, 101; **32**: 56, 155–6; **33**: 55–56, 99–100, 155–6; **34**: 99–100, 151–2; **35**: 97–98, 151–2; **36**: 97–98, 151–2; **37**: 95–96, 153–4; **38**: 97–98
Dower	1830s
	27: 154; **28**: 51–52

McDonald, Elizabeth L. and Helen B. "Guardianship Book A Found in Jefferson County Surrogate Court" *Jefferson County Genealogical Informer* 3 (1996): 7, 17; 4 (1997) 15, 39.

Samuelsen, W. David. *Jefferson County, New York Will Testators Index, 1830–1900*. Salt Lake City: Sampubco, 1996. ●FHL

Records on the Internet

New York GenWeb, Jefferson County
www.usgenweb.org
  Abstracts of select Jefferson County wills.

Sampubco
www.Sampubco.com
  Wills are indexed 1792 to 1917

US Genweb Archives Project
www.usgwarchives.org
  Includes the Sampubco indexes as well as abstracts of Intestate Records, Letters of Administration, Letters Testamentary, Court Contests, and Estate Appraisals.

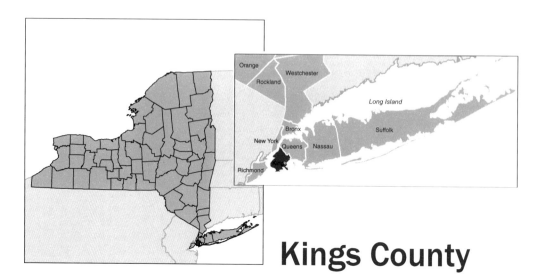

Kings County

Kings County Surrogate's Court

2 Johnson Street
Brooklyn, NY 11201

Phone   (347) 404–9700
Fax   (718) 643–6237
email   None
Hours   M–F 9:00 am to 5:00 pm
Website www.nycourts.gov/courts/2jd/index.shtml

Date Formed	1 November 1683
County Seat	Brooklyn
Parent County	Original

Special Notes

Original files to 1974 are stored in the basement. Patrons may request up to three per day. All requests must be made before 3:00 pm. Card indexes cover records up to 1992, after which estates are indexed on computer. Self–service copiers (35¢) are in the research room. Volumes of most of the early–recorded wills and some other recorded items are also in the room.

Early files are now scanned and available in the research room on CD-ROM. Many requests come back "missing," more than likely a problem with disorganized files in the basement.

Records on Microfilm at the Family History Library

Records		Indexes
Wills	1787–1915	1789–1971
Letters testamentary	1830–1865	
Probate proceedings	1829–1866	
Proceedings	1798–1909	
Unprobated Sealed Wills	1853–1864	
Administrations	1787–1866	1787–1903

Records (cont.)

Letters of Administration	1787–1923
Petitions and Orders of Administration	1817–1865
Petitions for Administrations with the Will Annexed	1857–1876
Letters of Guardianship	1814–1868
Guardianship records, petitions, affidavits, orders	1833–1865
Guardians annual accounts	1842–1865
Real Estate Proceedings	1798–1868
Real Estate Proceedings, Property Disposition for the Deceased	1868–1909
Decrees on Final Accounting,	1831–1870, 1915, index 1830–1898
Final Accountings	1830–1865
Inventories	1732–1923
Miscellaneous Probate Records	1842–1865
Probate Packets	N/A
Estate Files	1866–1923

Published Records and Indexes

Barber, Gertrude A. *Index, Probate of Wills, Kings County, New York, January 1, 1850 to December 31, 1890.* 3 vols. Typescript. New York [?], 1948; reprint, Salem, Mass.: Higginson Book Co., 1996. ●FHL ∎LOC ∎NYPL

Moorhouse, B-Ann, and Joseph Michael Silinonte. *Kings County, New York, Administration Proceedings 1817–1856: Abstracts of the Earliest Proceedings in the Kings County Surrogate's Court, Brooklyn.* New York: New York Genealogical and Biographical Society, 2006. ∎NYPL

New York Genealogical and Biographical Society. *New York Genealogical and Biographical Record.* New York, 1870–. ∎FHL ∎NEHGS ∎NYPL ∎NYSL

    Wills   17th century [select wills registered at Court of Sessions and Courts of Common Pleas]
                                   47: 161–70, 227–32

Thomas, Milton H., comp. *Index to the Wills, Administrations, and Guardianships of Kings County, New York, 1650–1850.* Washington, D.C.: Charles Shepard, 1926. ●FHL ∎NYPL

Van Buren, DeWitt, comp. "Abstracts of Wills of Kings County, Recorded at Brooklyn, New York" 6 vols. Typescript. 1941. ●FHL ∎LOC ∎NEHGS ∎NYPL

Records on the Internet

Family Search

www.FamilySearch.org
New York, Kings County Estate Files, 1866–1923

New England Historic Genealogical Society

www.AmericanAncestors.org
Abstracts of Wills, Administrations and Guardianships in NY State, 1787–1835 [database].[note: Eardley did not transcribe the Kings County records, so NEHGS included records abstracted by DeWitt Van Buren in "Abstracts of Wills of Kings County Recorded at Brooklyn, New York" (see above)].

Sampubco

www.Sampubco.com
Kings County wills from 1787 to 1835 are indexed.

US Genweb Archives Project

www.usgwarchives.org
Includes the Sampubco indexes as well as abstracts of Intestate Records, Letters of Administration, Letters Testamentary, Court Contests, and Estate Appraisals.

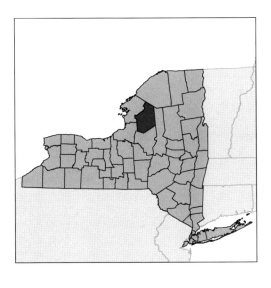

Lewis County

Lewis County Surrogate's Court

7660 State Street
Lowville, NY 13367

Phone	(315) 376–5344
Fax	(315) 376–1647
email	None
Hours	M–F 8:30 am to 4:30 pm (Sep–May)
	M–F 8:30 am to 4:00 pm (Jun–Aug)
Website	www.nycourts.gov/courts/5jd/lewis/surrogate/index.shtml

Date Formed	28 March 1805
County Seat	Lowville
Parent County	Oneida

Records on Microfilm at the Family History Library

Records		Indexes	
Wills	1806–1870	Surrogates Wills	1805–1940
Letters Testamentary & of Administration	1830–1855		
Letters of Administration	1805–1829, 1856–1881		
Letters of Guardianship	1806–1829		
Guardianship Records	1830–1855		
Admeasurement of Dower lands	1824–1866		
Final Settlement of Estates	1856–1883		
Probate Packets	N/A		

Published Records and Indexes

Central New York Genealogical Society. *Tree Talks.* Syracuse, N.Y., 1961–.
    ◆FHL ◆NEHGS ◆NYPL ◆NYSL

      Wills   1806–1838
                       13: 42, 162–3; **16**: 179–80; **17**: 97, 155–6; **18**: 103–4;
                       21: 107–8; **24**: 43–44; **28**: 53–54; **29**: 53–54; **30**: 51–52;

                    33: 102; **34**: 101–2; **35**: 99–100; **36**: 99–100; **37**: 97–98;
                    38: 99–100; **39**: 97–98; **40**: 97–98; **43**: 98; **44**: 97–98;
                    45: 93–94; **46**: 93–94; **47**: 97–98; **48**: 93–94; **49**: 43–44,
                    93–94
Guardianships   1806–1829
                    8: 152, 211; **9**: 38, 101; **23**: 46, 167–8
Administrations   1805–1829
                    30: 165–6; **31**: 51–52; **32**: 103–4; **33**: 101–2
Dower   1824–1845
                    13: 162–3; **14**: 45; **16**: 103–4; **24**: 167–8; **25**: 45

Samuelsen, W. David. *Lewis County, New York Will Testators Index, 1806–1870.* Salt Lake
    City: Sampubco, 1996. ●FHL

Records on the Internet

New England Historic Genealogical Society
www.AmericanAncestors.org
    Abstracts of Wills, Administrations and Guardianships in NY State, 1787–1835
    [database].

New York GenWeb, Lewis County
www.usgenweb.org
    Lewis County Will Book Indices Volumes C & D (1840–1862);
    Abstracts of select Lewis County wills.

Sampubco
www.Sampubco.com
    Lewis County wills from 1806 to 1870 are indexed.

US Genweb Archives Project
www.usgwarchives.org
    Includes the Sampubco indexes as well as abstracts of Intestate Records, Letters of
    Administration, Letters Testamentary, Court Contests, and Estate Appraisals.

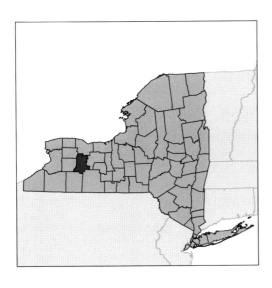

Livingston County

Livingston County Surrogate's Court
2 Court Street
Geneseo, NY 14454

Phone   (585) 243–7095
Fax   (585) 243–7583
email   tmoore@courts.state.ny.us
Hours   M–F 9:00 am to 5:00 pm
Website   www.rootsweb.com/~nyliving/repositories/clerk.htm
             www.nycourts.gov/courts/7jd/courts/surrogates

Date Formed	23 February 1821
County Seat	Geneseo
Parent County	Genesee

Records on Microfilm at the Family History Library

Records		Indexes	
Wills	1821–1905	Surrogates	1821–1931
Letters of Testamentary & of Administration	1830–1857		
Letters Testamentary	1861–1904		
Administrations	1830–1904		
Letters of Administration	1857–1904		
Guardianship Records	1823–1870		
Letters of Guardianship	1876–1915		
Orders & Decrees	1824–1916		
Probate Packets	N/A		

Published Records and Indexes

Central New York Genealogical Society. *Tree Talks.* Syracuse, N.Y., 1961–.
    ❙FHL ❙NEHGS ❙NYPL ❙NYSL

Wills	1820–1835
	4: 142, 198; **5**: 26, 77, 130; **14**: 47–48, 171–2; **15**: 53;
	28: 106; **29**: 105–6; **30**: 103; **31**: 103–4; **32**: 105–6;
	33: 103–4; **34**: 103–4; **35**: 101–2; **36**: 101–2; **37**: 99–100
Administrations	1821–1844
	38: 101–2; **39**: 99–100; **40**: 99–100; **41**: 101–2; **42**: 99–100;
	43: 99–100; **44**: 99–100; **45**: 95–96

Records on the Internet

New England Historic Genealogical Society

www.AmericanAncestors.org
> Abstracts of Wills, Administrations and Guardianships in NY State, 1787–1835 [database].

Sampubco

www.Sampubco.com
> Livingston County wills from 1821 to 1905 are indexed.

US Genweb Archives Project

www.usgwarchives.org
> Includes the Sampubco indexes as well as abstracts of Intestate Records, Letters of Administration, Letters Testamentary, Court Contests, and Estate Appraisals.

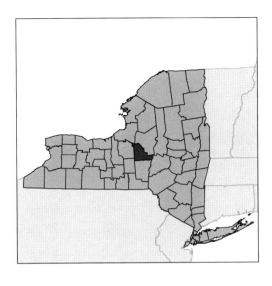

Madison County

Madison County Surrogate's Court
138 North Court Street
Wampsville, NY 13163

Mailing Address
PO Box 607
Wampsville, NY 13163

Phone   (315) 366–2392
Fax   (315) 366–2539
email   None
Hours   M–F 9:00 am to 5:00 pm
Website www.nycourts.gov/courts/6jd/madison/surrogate.shtml

Date Formed   21 March 1806
County Seat   Wampsville
Parent County Chenango

Special Notes

Microfilm copies of original records for 1806–1970 are available for searches at the office. The original records are stored in another facility and are not accessible to the public.

Records on Microfilm at the Family History Library

Records		Indexes	
Wills	1806–1900	Estates	1806–1920
Letters Testamentary	1847–1870	Surrogates Office	1890–1919
Letters of Administration	1830–1903	Admin Index	1806–1890
Administration Bonds	1890–1903		
Letters of Administration, with the Will Annexed	1890–1927	Index	1806–1890
Register and Index of Bonds and Undertakings	1889–1901		
Letters of Guardianship	1808–1927	Guardians	1806–1890
Guardian Books	1890–1904		

Records (cont.)		Indexes (cont.)	
Guardianship Papers	1806–1900		
Book of Dower	1830–1880[2]		
Estate Files	1806–1876		
	(indexed by Sampubco)		
Minutes, Orders, & Decrees	1830–1902		
Miscellaneous Minutes,			
Orders and Decrees	1854–1900		
Probate of Heirship	1893–1925		
Judicial Settlements	1830–1846,	Index	1806–1890
	1856–1900		
Probate Packets	See Estate Files		

Published Records and Indexes

Central New York Genealogical Society. *Tree Talks.* Syracuse, N.Y., 1961–.
❚FHL ❚NEHGS ❚NYPL ❚NYSL

Wills	1808–1828
	9: 39, 102, 230; **10**: 43, 105, 169, 243; **12**: 202; **13**: 43–44, 82–83, 166–7; **15**: 56, 131–2, 209–10; **16**: 27–28, 105; **17**: 99–100, 159–60; **18**: 43–44, 105–6; **21**: 111–2, 165–6; **22**: 39–40, 113, 169; **27**: 107–8, 155–6; **28**: 55–56, 107–8, 153–4; **30**: 105–6, 167–8; **31**: 53–54, 105–6, 155–6; **32**: 57
Administrations	1808–1828
	2: 10, 30, 50, 74; **3**: 17, 52, 90, 122; **4**: 35, 86, 143, 199; **5**: 27, 78, 131, 182; **6**: 32, 84, 127, 174; **7**: 38, 93, 146, 200; **8**: 35, 96, 154, 213
Dower Proceedings	1830–1880
	14: 84, 173–4; **15**: 55

Records on the Internet

New England Historic Genealogical Society

www.AmericanAncestors.org

Abstracts of Wills, Administrations and Guardianships in NY State, 1787–1835 [database].

New York GenWeb, Madison County

www.usgenweb.org

Madison County Will Book Indices Volumes C & D (1840 – 1862); Abstracts of select Madison County wills.

---

[2] Miscatalogued as Monroe County, but still listed under Madison County – Probate Records.

Sampubco

www.Sampubco.com

Madison County wills from 1806 to 1900 are indexed.

US Genweb Archives Project

www.usgwarchives.org/ny/madison/wills/willstoc.htm

Includes the Sampubco indexes as well as abstracts of Intestate Records, Letters of Administration, Letters Testamentary, Court Contests, and Estate Appraisals.

Monroe County

Monroe County Surrogate's Court

99 Exchange Blvd.
Room 541, Hall of Justice
Rochester, NY 14614

Phone	(585) 428–5200
Fax	(212) 295–4922
email	mannunzi@courts.state.ny.us
Hours	M–F 9:00 am to 5:00 pm
Website	www.nycourts.gov/courts/7jd/courts/surrogates

Date Formed	23 February 1821
County Seat	Rochester
Parent County	Genesee/Ontario

Special Notes

Most records are stored offsite. Make arrangements in advance to review records at the office.

Records on Microfilm at the Family History Library

Records		Indexes	
Wills	1829–1901	Surrogates	1821–1970[3]
Letters Testamentary	1864–1901		
Letter of Administration	1863–1901		
Letters of Guardianship	1826–1902		
Probate Packets	N/A		
Miscellaneous Records			
(Surrogates)	1865–1902		
Miscellaneous Record Index			
(County Clerk)	1821–1923		

[3] There are two indexes: the General Index and the General Record Index (both 1821–1970). The General Index, which gives a file number, and should be checked first. The General Record Index gives specific volume and page numbers.

Published Records and Indexes

Barber, Gertrude A. *Monroe County, New York Abstracts of Wills: Copied from the Original Records at Rochester, New York, [1821–1847].* 2 vols. Typescript. New York [?], 1941. ●FHL ▪LOC ▪NEHGS ▪NYPL ▪NYSL

Card, Lester L., comp. "Monroe County Surrogate Records, N.Y." Typescript. ●FHL

Clark, Francis. "Persons Mentioned by Name in Early Probated Wills in Monroe County, NY" *Yesteryears* 34 (1991): 89.

Central New York Genealogical Society. *Tree Talks.* Syracuse, N.Y., 1961–.
▪FHL ▪NEHGS ▪NYPL ▪NYSL

Wills	1821–1853, Pre 1863–1874
	3: 18, 53, 91, 123; **4**: 36, 87, 144, 200; **5**: 28, 79, 132, 183;
	6: 33, 85, 128, 175; **7**: 39, 94, 147, 201; **8**: 36, 97, 155, 214;
	9: 40, 103, 168, 231; **10**: 44, 106, 170, 245; **17**: 37–38;
	19: 41–42; **20**: 47–48, 175–6; **21**: 167–8
Intestates:	Pre 1863
	11: 51–52, 171–2; **12**: 49–50, 169–70; **13**: 45–46, 168–9;
	17: 36–37; **21**: 41–42; **22**: 41
Guardianships	1801–1853
	13: 169; **14**: 51–52, 175–6; **15**: 57–58, 211–2; **17**: 35–36;
	44: 103–4; **45**: 99–100; **46**: 99–100; **47**: 103–4; **48**: 99–100;
	49: 99–100

Cohen, Minnie, comp. *Abstracts of Wills of Monroe County, N.Y.: from 1821–1841.* Imprint: 1941.

Daughters of the American Revolution Magazine. Washington, D.C., 1913–.

Wills	1821–1860

Early Rochester Records, Vol. 2. [Microfilm of newspaper clippings at the New York State Library, Albany, New York. Contains Monroe County Revolutionary War veterans' records; Monroe County probate records; Rochester church, vital, and cemetery records. All the records are apparently from Rochester newspapers.]

Haynes, Myrte Rice. "Settlements of Estates of Early Residents in Monroe County, New York," in Janet Wethy Foley, *Early Settlers of New York State.* 2 vols. 1934–1942; reprint, Baltimore, Md.: Genealogical Publishing Co., 1993. Vol. 2, pp. 361, 377, 393, 409, 425, 441, 458, 473, 489. [Estates of Monroe County residents in Genesee and Ontario Counties before Monroe was created in 1821].

Irondequoit Chapter. "Unpublished Intestate Estates, Monroe Co., NY." *New York DAR Genealogical Records Committee Report,* series 1, volume 51 (1932). ▪DAR

———. "Unpublished Records from Monroe County Cemetery Inscriptions and Cross Indexes of Wills and Intestate Estates Together With Orleans County Cemetery Inscriptions." New York DAR Genealogical Records Committee Report, Series 1, volume 64 (n.d.). ▪DAR

———. "Unpublished Wills of Monroe Co., NY, 1821–1860." *New York DAR Genealogical Records Committee Report,* series 1, volume 52 (1932).

Records on the Internet

New England Historic Genealogical Society
www.AmericanAncestors.org
> Abstracts of Wills, Administrations and Guardianships in NY State, 1787–1835 [database].

Sampubco
www.Sampubco.com
> Monroe County wills from 1806 to 1900 are indexed.

US Genweb Archives Project
www.usgwarchives.org/ny/monroe/wills/willstoc.htm
> Includes the Sampubco indexes as well as abstracts of Intestate Records, Letters of Administration, Letters Testamentary, Court Contests, and Estate Appraisals.

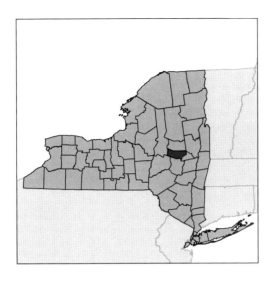

Montgomery County

Montgomery County Surrogate's Court

58 Broadway
PO Box 1500
Fonda, NY 12068

Phone   (518) 853–8108
Fax   (518) 853–8230
email   None
Hours   M–F 9:00 am to 5:00 pm
Website   www.nycourts.gov/courts/4jd/montgomery/index.shtml

Date Formed	12 March 1772
County Seat	Fonda
Parent County	Albany (created as Tryon; name changed 1784)

Records on Microfilm at the Family History Library

Records		Indexes	
Wills	1810–1919	General	1787–1905
Letters Testamentary	1862–1920		
Letters of Administrations	1788–1921		
Bonds	1890–1899		
Orders of Administration	1896–1909		
Guardianship Letters	1825–1922		
Index, Guardian Reports	1825–1862		
Orders & Decrees	1802–1918		
Orders of Probate	1874–1922		
Probate Packets	N/A		

Published Records and Indexes

Becker, Edith V., comp. "Abstracts and Indexes For Volumes I and II of Montgomery County, New York, Wills, 1782–1838." Typescript. ●FHL

——. "Inventories, Montgomery County, New York, 1795–1800." Typescript. ●FHL

Central New York Genealogical Society. *Tree Talks*. Syracuse, N.Y., 1961–.
∎FHL ∎NEHGS ∎NYPL ∎NYSL

Wills	1787–1810
	25: 172; **26**: 111–2; **27**: 111–2; **28**: 111–2
Administrations	1788–1808
	21: 170; **24**: 169; **28**: 112; **29**: 111–2; **30**: 109–10;
	31: 109–10; **32**: 111–2
Guardianships	1825–1838
	33: 109–10; **34**: 109–10; **35**: 107–8; **36**: 107–8; **37**: 105–6;
	38: 107–8; **39**: 105–6; **40**: 105–6; **41**: 107; **46**: 102;
	47: 53–54, 105–6; **48**: 53–54, 101–2; **49**: 47–48, 101–2
Dower	1808–1876
	12: 171–2; **13**: 47–48, 170; **20**: 113–4, 177–8; **21**: 43–44,
	169; **24**: 170

New York Genealogical and Biographical Society. *New York Genealogical and Biographical Record*. New York, 1870–. ∎FHL ∎NEHGS ∎NYPL ∎NYSL

Wills	1787–1831
	56: 145–61, 380–97; **57**: 163–86, 264–82.
Intestates	1784–1787
	59: 83–85.

The Mohawk. Rhinebeck, N.Y.: Kinship, 1984–1998. ∎FHL ∎NEHGS ∎NYPL ∎NYSL

Letters of Admin.	1788–1807
	1: 23–26, 46–48.
Guardianships Index	1825–1829
	9: 65–68, 75–78, 118

Records on the Internet

New England Historic Genealogical Society
www.AmericanAncestors.org
Abstracts of Wills, Administrations and Guardianships in NY State, 1787–1835 [database].

New York GenWeb, Herkimer County
www.usgenweb.com
Abstracts of select Montgomery County wills on the Herkimer/ Montgomery Counties Wills and Deeds Bulletin Boards.

Sampubco
www.Sampubco.com
Montgomery County wills from 1787 to 1918 are indexed.

US Genweb Archives Project
www.usgwarchives.org/ny/montgomery/wills/willstoc.htm
Includes the Sampubco indexes as well as abstracts of Intestate Records, Letters of Administration, Letters Testamentary, Court Contests, and Estate Appraisals.

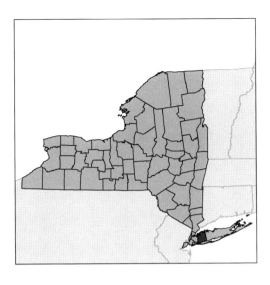

Nassau County

Nassau County Surrogate's Court

262 Old Country Road
Mineola, NY 11501

Phone	(516) 571–2082
	(516) 571–2847
Fax	(516) 571–3803
email	None
Hours	M–F 9:00 am to 5:00 pm (unpredictable closings, call ahead)
Website	www.nycourts.gov/courts/10jd/nassau/surrogates.shtml

Date Formed	27 April 1898
County Seat	Mineola
Parent County	Queens

Special Notes

The staff recommends that researchers arrive by 4 pm. All requests must be submitted prior to 4:30 pm. All files must be returned by 4:35 pm. Older files are stored in the basement. Staff retrieves files from the basement twice a day, at 11 am and 2 pm. Limit of five file requests per day.

Records on Microfilm at the Family History Library

None

Published Records and Indexes

None

Records on the Internet

None

New York County

New York County Surrogate's Court

31 Chambers Street
New York, NY 10007

Mailing Address

New York County Surrogate's Court
Attn: Record Search
31 Chambers Street
New York, NY 10007

Phone	(646) 386–5000
Fax	(212) 374–3250
email	None
Hours	M–F 9:00 am to 5:00 pm
Website	www.nycourts.gov/courts/1jd/surrogate

Date Formed	1 November 1683
County Seat	New York City
Parent County	Original

New York City Municipal Archives

31 Chambers Street, Room 103
New York, NY 10007

Phone	(212) 639–9675
Fax	None
email	None
Hours	M–Th 9:00 am to 5:00 pm, F 9:00 am to 1:00 p.m.
Website	www.nyc.gov/html/records/html/about/archives.shtml

Special Notes

All indexes are in Room 402. Pre-1950 indexes (previously on microfilm), and book indexes from 1964 to the present have been scanned and can be browsed on computers. The period 1950 to 1963 is available in the same room on a card index. Book indexes for inventories, guardianships, and accountings are behind the counter.

Many probate files available on microfilm, as well as files from 1964 to 1968 and 1980, are scanned and available on computers. Original pre-1964 files are stored off-site. It may take two weeks or longer for the files to be delivered.

Original papers for early estates are filed chronologically by type of document, not alphabetically by decedent.

The Municipal Archives holds original inventories from ca. 1783 to 1844 in Room 103. Original wills for 1787–1829 from New York County Surrogate's Court are at the New York State Archives in Albany.

Records on Microfilm at the Family History Library

Records		Indexes	
Wills	1665–1916	Surrogates Wills	1662–1923
Wills Mayors Court	1805–1824		
Wills Supreme Court	1787–1927		
Executors Renunciations	1792–1890	Index	1830–1912
Orders Admitting Wills	1851–1866		
Orders Granting and Denying Petitions	1828–1865	Index	1830–1882
Letters Testamentary	1793–1806		
Letters Testamentary	1830–1866		
Probate Proceedings	1830–1865		
Letters of Administration	1743–1866	Index	1743–1910
Letters and Petitions of Administration	1798–1862		
Petitions for Letters of administrations Administration Bonds	1753–1866		
Record of Dower	1831–1856		
Inventories	1862–1865		
Proceedings and Orders	1800–1882		
Accounts not in Decrees	1810–1862		
Decrees on Accounting	1828–1865	Indexes	1828–1907
Inventories	1862–1865		
Miscellaneous Orders	1803–1870		
Miscellaneous Probate Records	1800–1869		
Petitions and Accounts	1803–1888		
Estate Orders	1840–1865		
Letters of Collection	1858–1865		
Special Collection Bonds	1849–1870		
Real Estate Proceedings	1800–1880		
Proceedings to Probate Wills of Real Estate	1830–1867		

Records (cont.)		Indexes (cont.)	
Proceedings in the			
Sale of Real Estate	1800–1872	Index	1800–1872
Probate Packets	See Special Notes		

Published Records and Indexes

Barber, Gertrude A., comp., *Abstracts of Wills of New York County, March 22, 1850 to April 1856, Copied from the Original Records at the Hall of Records, New York City*. 5 vols. Typescript. New York [?]: Gertrude A. Barber, 1950–1960.

———. *Index to Letters of Administration of New York County, 1743–1875*. 6 vols. Typescript. New York [?]: Gertrude A. Barber, 1951. ●FHL

Central New York Genealogical Society. *Tree Talks*. Syracuse, N.Y., 1961–.
■FHL ■NEHGS ■NYPL ■NYSL

Guardianships   1838

Freeman, Paul, abst. *Selected Wills from the New York County Surrogate's Records*. Typescript, 1940). [Contains wills of Amerman, Bedell, Carman, Concklin/Conklin, Creed, Demott/Demotte, Denton, Ditmas, Hallock, Hendrickson, Lefferts, Mott, Norton, Pearsall, Ryerson, Valentine, Van Cleef, Van Wyck, Weeks, Wells, Wright, and Wyckoff families.] ●FHL

Kelly, Arthur C. M., comp. *Index, Names of Principals [to] Abstracts of Wills, 1665–1776, on File in the Surrogate's Office, City of New York*. New York: New York Historical Society, 1892–1899; reprint, Rhinebeck, N.Y.: Palatine Transcripts, 1981.

———. *Index, Names of Principals [to] Abstracts of Wills, 1777–1800, on File in the Surrogate's Office, City of New York*. New York: New York Historical Society, 1900–1906; reprint, Rhinebeck, N.Y.: Palatine Transcripts, 1981.

Scott, Kenneth. "Appointment of Guardians, Mayor's Court, New York City" [1695–1742], *National Genealogical Society Quarterly*. 56 (1968): 51–53.
■FHL ■NEHGS ■NYPL ■NYSL

———. "Old New York Inventories of Estates" *The New York Historical Society Quarterly Bulletin* 4 (1922–23): 130–37. ■NEHGS ■NYPL ■NYSL

Inventories   1719–1800

Post, John J., comp. *Index of Wills Proved in the Supreme Court, Court of Common Pleas, County Court, and Court of Probate, and on File in the Office of the Clerk of the Court of Appeals*. New York: S. Victor Constant, 1899. ●FHL

Sawyer, Ray C., comp. *Abstracts of Wills for New York County, New York, 1808–1814*. 2 vols. Typescript, 1934. [Actually covers 1801–1814. Ray Sawyer apparently abstracted wills through 1849, but the FHL does not have the volumes after 1814.] ●FHL

————. *Abstracts of Wills Probated in the Common Pleas Court (also known as Mayor's Court), 1817–1892; Supreme Court of Judicature, 1821–1829; Supreme Court of the Judicature 1847–1856; Supreme Court of the Judicature 1856–1870, all of New York County, New York City, New York.* Typescript, 1948. ●FHL ▌NYPL

————. *Index of Wills for New York County* (New York City), 1662–1850. 3 vols. Typescript, 1930. ●FHL

————. *Index to Wills for New York County, New York, 1851–1875.* 3 vols. Typescript, 1950. ●FHL

Vail, Alfred, comp. *Copies of Records of New York Surrogate's Court, New York City, 1823, etc.* Typescript, 1941. [Deals with Vail family wills from the 1700s to 1800s.] ●FHL

Washburn, Georgia, C., comp. *Index of Wills on File in the Surrogate's Office, Hall of Records, New York, New York, for the Years 1801–1820.* n.p., 1937.

Records on the Internet

New England Historic Genealogical Society
www.AmericanAncestors.org

Abstracts of Wills, Administrations and Guardianships in NY State, 1787–1835 [database].

Includes only wills in the Supreme Court of New York County, not those in the Surrogate's Court.

Sampubco
www.Sampubco.com

New York County wills from 1655 to 1840 are indexed.

US Genweb Archives Project
www.usgwarchives.org

Includes the Sampubco indexes to 1825, as well as abstracts of some wills.

Niagara County

Niagara County Surrogate's Court

Niagara County Courthouse
175 Hawley Street
Lockport, NY 14094

Date Formed	11 March 1808
County Seat	Lockport
Parent County	Genesee

Phone	(716) 439–7130
Fax	(716) 439–7319
email	None
Hours	M–F 9:00 am to 5:00 pm
Website	www.nycourts.gov/courts.8jd/Niagara/index.shtml

Records on Microfilm at the Family History Library

Records		Indexes	
Wills	1840–1901	Surrogates	1822–1928
Letters testamentary	1820–1906		
Administrations	1820–1906		
Appointment of Guardians	1831–1965	Guardians	1830–1972
Letters of Guardianship	1839–1902		
Bonds of Guardians	1890–1904		
Judical settlements of guardianship	1881–1928		
Final settlements of guardianship	1919–1935		
Guardianship Papers in boxes by first letter of surname	arranged alphabetically		
Probate Records	1930–1971		
Probate Records (loose) arranged alphabetically in boxes by first letter of surname	1835–1970		

Records (cont.)

Minutes, orders, and decrees	1820–1906
Final Settlements	1820–1906
Real Estate	1820–1906
Probate Packets	See Probate Records (loose)

Published Records and Indexes

Central New York Genealogical Society. *Tree Talks.* Syracuse, N.Y., 1961–.
∎FHL ∎NEHGS ∎NYPL ∎NYSL

Estate Records	1812–1821
	3: 124; **4**: 38, 89, 146, 202; **5**: 29, 81, 134, 185
Guardianships	1831–1844
	6: 35, 87, 129, 177; **19**: 43–44; **20**:115–6; **36**: 110;
	37: 107–108; **38**: 109–110; **39**: 107–8; **40**: 107–8;
	41: 109–10; **42**: 107–8; **43**: 107–8; **44**: 107–8; **45**: 104,
	151–2; **46**: 103–4; **47**: 107–8, 151–2; **48**: 103–4, 151–2
Wills	**21**: 113–4; **22**: 115–6; **23**: 111

Niagara County Genealogical Society Newsletter. Lockport, N.Y.: Niagara County
Genealogical Society, 1979—.

Wills and Probate	1800–1840
	7: (No. 3), (No. 4); **8**: (No. 2); **9**: (No. 1) 9–10, (No. 2) 9–10

Western New York Genealogical Society. *Western New York Genealogical Society Journal.*
Hamburg, N.Y, 1974–. ∎FHL ∎NEHGS ∎NYPL ∎NYSL

Wills Index	through 1880
	6: 6–23, 61–73, 124–33

Clapsattle, Gertrude Starkey. "Niagara County, New York Wills Index 1828 to 1860."
New York DAR Genealogical Records Committee Report, series 1, volume 456 (1977).
∎DAR ∎NYPL

Records on the Internet

New England Historic Genealogical Society
www.AmericanAncestors.org
Abstracts of Wills, Administrations and Guardianships in NY State, 1787–1835
[database].

Sampubco
www.Sampubco.com
Niagara County wills from 1818 to 1901 are indexed.

US Genweb Archives Project
www.usgwarchives.org
Includes the Sampubco indexes as well as abstracts of some wills.

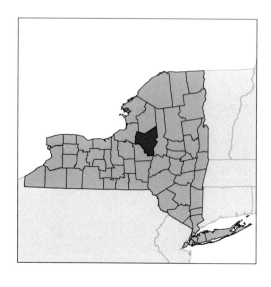

Oneida County

Oneida County Surrogate's Court

Oneida County Office Building
800 Park Avenue, 8th floor
Utica, NY 13501

Phone	(315) 266–4550
Fax	(315) 797–9237
email	None
Hours	M–F 8:30 am to 4:30 pm (Sep–Jun)
	M–F 8:30 am. to 4:00 pm (Jul–Aug)
Website	www.nycourts.gov/courts/5jd/oneida/index.shtml

Date Formed	15 March 1798
County Seat	Utica, Rome
Parent County	Herkimer

Records on Microfilm at the Family History Library

Records

Wills	1798–1900
Administrators bonds	1893–1900
Guardianships	1871–1903
Guardianship letters	1844–1889
Guardian Records	alphabetically arranged
Index to guardianship papers which are filed in boxes and numbered A1–A2866	
Misc. Guardians Records	1830–1898
Guardians Accounts & Bonds	1884–1901
Executors and Administrators accounts	1830–1900
Petitions, Administrators Bonds, oaths to inventory and other loose papers	1870–1875

Indexes

Surrogates Wills	1798–1909
Guardian	1870–1933

Records (cont.)

Probate Proceedings	1867–1965
Notices to heirs and deceased soldiers concerning appointments of guardians and other probate matters	from approx. 1800
Appraisal letters	1856–1891
Probate Packets	See Probate Proceedings

Published Records and Indexes

Barber, Gertrude A., comp. *Abstracts of Wills, of Oneida County, New York, 1798–1848.* 6 vols. in 3. Typescript. New York, 1939. ●FHL ▮LOC ▮NEHGS ▮NYPL ▮NYSL

Barber, Gertrude A, comp. *Index of Wills of Oneida County, New York.* New York, 1939. ▮LOC

Central New York Genealogical Society. *Tree Talks.* Syracuse, N.Y., 1961–. ▮FHL ▮NEHGS ▮NYPL ▮NYSL

Wills	1798–1830s
	24: 47–48; **39**: 109–10, 153–4; **40**: 57; **43**: 58, 109–10, 153–4; **44**: 57–58, 109–10, 153–4; **45**: 55–56, 105–6, 153–4; **46**: 55–56, 105–6, 151–2; **47**: 55–56, 109–10, 153–4; **48**: 55–56, 105–6, 153–4; **49**: 49–50, 103–6, 151–2
Administrations	1798–1817
	22: 44, 117–8, 173–4; **23**: 113–4, 171–2; **25**: 50, 109–10, 173–4; **26**: 57–58; **32**: 59–60, 115–6, 159–60; **33**: 59–60, 113–4, 159–60; **34**: 57–58; **38**: 112, 155–156; **39**: 57–58, 109
Guardianships	1843–1846
	41: 111–2, 153–4; **42**: 57–58, 109–10, 153–4; **43**: 57–58
Minutes	1836
	18: 45–46

Samuelsen, W. David. *Oneida County, New York Will Testators Index, 1798–1900.* Salt Lake City: Sampubco, 1996. ●FHL

Records on the Internet

New England Historic Genealogical Society
www.AmericanAncestors.org
Abstracts of Wills, Administrations and Guardianships in NY State, 1787–1835 [database].

New York GenWeb, Oneida County
www.usgenweb.org
"Abstracts of Wills 1798–1848." Uncredited, but email address of the contributor is *nyoneida@yahoo.com*). These appear to be images of typewritten abstracts by Gertrude Barber (see above), but are not credited as such.

Sampubco

www.Sampubco.com

Oneida County wills are indexed 1795 to 1888.

US Genweb Archives Project

www.usgwarchives.org

Includes the Sampubco indexes, as well as abstracts of some wills.

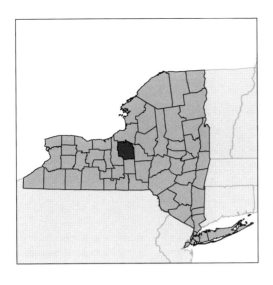

Onondaga County

Onondaga County Surrogate's Court

401 Montgomery St
Syracuse, NY 13202–2173

Phone	(315) 671–2100
Fax	(315) 671–1162
email	None
Hours	M–F 8:30 am to 4:30 pm (Sep–May)
	M–F 8:30 am to 4:00 pm (Jun–Jul)
Website	www.nycourts.gov/courts/5jd/onondaga/surrogate

Date Formed	5 March 1794
County Seat	Syracuse
Parent County	Herkimer

Records on Microfilm at the Family History Library

Records		Indexes	
Wills	1796–1867	Surrogates	1802–1923
Letters Testamentary			
& Letters of Administration	1830–1852		
Letters Testamentary	1852–1867		
Administrations	1830–1866		
Letters of Administration	1852–1866		
Appointment of Guardians	1824–1873	Guardians	1824–1960
Letters of Guardianship			
and Proceedings			
of Real Estate	1824–1829		
Proceedings in Dower	1830–1879		
Proceedings, Disposition			
of Real Estate	1831–1881		
Misc Orders & Decrees	1821–1868		

Records (cont.)

Court records of Onondaga County, New York Abstracts of Appointments of Guardianship, Letters of Administration	1821–1852
Probate Packets	N/A

Published Records and Indexes

Card, Lester L., comp. *Onondaga Surrogate Records, 1795–1842.* 6 vols. Typescript, 1941. ●FHL ▮NYPL

Card, Lester L., comp. *Vital Records of Onondaga County and Other Localities in the State of New York, 1795–1913.* 6 vols. Typescript, 1941. ●FHL ▮NYPL

Central New York Genealogical Society. *Tree Talks.* Syracuse, N.Y., 1961–. ▮FHL ▮NEHGS ▮NYPL ▮NYSL

Wills	1794–1828
	7: 42, 97, 150, 205; **8**: 39, 101, 159, 218; **9**: 44, 107; **29**: 60, 117–8, 159–60; **30**: 59; **32**: 61–62, 117–8, 161–2; **33**: 162; **34**: 59–60, 115–6, 157–8; **35**: 61–62, 113–4, 157–8; **36**: 61–62, 113–4, 157–8; **37**: 61–62, 111–2, 159–60; **38**: 61–62
Administrations	1794–1816
	4: 91, 148, 204; **5**: 31, 83; **11**: 89–90, 175–6, 209
Guardianships	1817–1829
	5: 83, 136, 187; **6**: 37, 89; **11**: 210; **12**: 51; **42**: 112, 155–6; **43**: 59–60, 111–2, 155–6; **44**: 59–60, 111–2, 155–6
Dower	1814–1816, 1830–1849
	9: 44; **10**: 48, 110, 174, 253; **11**: 55–56

Coleman, Minnie L. C. "Abstracts of Wills, Surrogate's Office, Onondaga County, New York, 1796–1841." 5 vols. Typescript, 1934–1940. ●FHL ▮NEHGS

———. "Appointment of Guardians, May 31, 1824–December 30, 1829. From the Original Records Book 'A,' Surrogate's Office, Court House, Onondaga County, New York." Syracuse, 1934. ▮NEHGS

———. "Appointment of Guardians, Book 'B,' Surrogate's Office, Onondaga County, New York. Abstracted from the Original Book 'B' Feby 1830–Dec 1836." Syracuse, 1934. ▮NEHGS

———. "Appointment of Guardians, Book 'B,' Surrogate's Office, Onondaga County, New York. Abstracted from the Original Book 'B' Feby 1830–Dec 1836. Part II: Being pages 236–418 from the Original Book." Syracuse, 1934. ▮NEHGS

——. "Appointment of Guardians, Book 'C,' Surrogate's Office, Onondaga County at Syracuse, New York. November 13th 1840 to March 9,1849." Syracuse, 1934. *∥*NEHGS

——. "Appointment of Guardians, Book 'CC,' March 15, 1849–December 1,1849." Syracuse, 1935. *∥*NEHGS

——. "Letters of Administration, Surrogates Office Onondaga county court house, Syracuse, New York, Books 1–5, 1795–1822." Typescript, 1933. ●FHL

——. "Letters of Guardianship, Surrogate's Office, Onondaga County, New York, December 1815 to March 1824. Copied from the Records in Book #3." Syracuse, 1933. *∥*NEHGS

——. "Letters of Guardianship Book 'A,' Years: April 1824 to December 1829." Syracuse, 1933. *∥*NEHGS

——. "Surrogate's Office of Onandaga County, Syracuse, New York Book 3, Old Records, Appointments of Guardians 1803–1815." Syracuse, 1936. *∥*NEHGS

Onondaga County, New York Wills. 3 vols. Sauk Village, Ill.: Hanson Heritage Pub., 1981–1982. ●FHL *∥*LOC *∥*NYPL *∥*NYSL

Samuelsen, W. David. *Onondaga County, New York Will Testators Index, 1796–1867.* Salt Lake City: Sampubco, 1996. ●FHL

Records on the Internet

New England Historic Genealogical Society
www.AmericanAncestors.org

Abstracts of Wills, Administrations and Guardianships in NY State, 1787–1835 [database].

Abstracts of Wills in Onondaga County, New York, 1791–1841 [From Minnie L. C. Coleman typescript above].

Onondaga County, NY: Guardianship Records, 1815–1849 [From Minnie L.C. Coleman typescripts at NEHGS above].

Sampubco
www.Sampubco.com

Onandaga wills from 1796 to 1867 are indexed 1796 to 1867.

US Genweb Archives Project
www.usgwarchives.org

Includes abstracts of some wills.

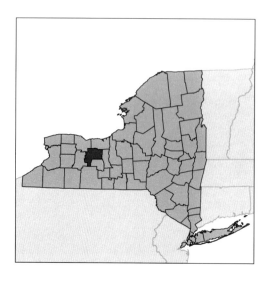

Ontario County

Ontario County Surrogate's Court

27 North Main Street
Canandaigua, NY 14424

Phone	(585) 396–4812
Fax	(585) 396–4576
email	esimpson@courts.state.ny.us
Hours	M–F 9:00 am to 5:00 pm
Website	www.nycourts.gov/courts/7jd/courts/surrogates

Date Formed	27 January 1789
County Seat	Canandaigua
Parent County	Montgomery

Ontario County Dept. of Records, Archives, and Information Management Services (RAIMS)

3051 County Complex Drive
Canandaigua, NY 14424

Phone	(585) 396–4376
Fax	None
email	None
Hours	M–F 9:00 am to 4:30 pm
Website	http://raims.com

Special Notes

Ontario County RAIMS is now the official repository for all pre-1930 records previously held by the Ontario County Surrogate's Court. Before contacting either the County Clerk or the County Surrogate, genealogists should contact the RAIMS to determine the current location of records.

RAIMS is a showcase for record management in New York State. Housed in a climate controlled building, researchers are required to wear cotton gloves (provided by the facility) and use only pencils. The staff provides research services for an hourly fee. RAIMS publishes a "Researcher's Guide," provided upon request.

Records on Microfilm at the Family History Library

Records		Indexes	
Record of Wills	1795–1924	Surrogates	1789–1965
Proofs of Wills	1858–1866		
Letters Testamentary and of Administration	1830–1857		
Record of Guardians	1814–1817		
Records & Letters of Guardians	1830–1876		
Inventories (filmed at Ontario Co. Historical Society)	1797–1822		
Record of Orders	1862–1874		
Record of Real Estate	1851–1883		
Probate Records	1818–1924		
Probate Packets	N/A		

Published Records and Indexes

Central New York Genealogical Society. *Tree Talks.* Syracuse, N.Y., 1961–.
❙FHL ❙NEHGS ❙NYPL ❙NYSL

Letters of Administration	1795–1798
	11: 92
Wills	1794–1808, 1830–1831
	10: 49, 111, 175; **19**: 177–8; **22**: 47, 48, 175–6; **23**: 51–52; **24**: 51–52; **25**: 53, 54; **26**: 119–20, 161; **27**: 119–20, 161–2; **28**: 119–10, 159–60; **29**: 119–20; **38**: 115–6, 159–60; **39**: 113–4, 157–8; **40**: 113–14, 157–8; **41**: 115–6, 157–8; **42**: 113–4, 157–8; **43**: 113–4, 157; **44**: 157–8; **45**: 109–10, 157–8; **46**: 109–10, 155–6; **47**: 113–4, 157–8; **48**: 109–10, 157–8; **49**: 109, 110, 157–8

Haynes, Myrte Rice. "Settlements of Estates of Early Residents in Monroe County, New York," in Janet Wethy Foley, *Early Settlers of New York State*. 1934–1942; reprint 2 vols., Baltimore: Genealogical Publishing Co., 1993. Vol. 2, pp. 361, 377, 393, 409, 425, 441, 458, 473, 489. ❙FHL ❙NEHGS

Wiles, Harriett M. *Abstracts of Wills of Ontario County, New York: in the Courthouse, Canandaigua, N.Y., 1794–1834.* 2 vols. Typescript, 1942. ●FHL ❙NYPL ❙NYSL

Records on the Internet

New England Historic Genealogical Society
www.AmericanAncestors.org
Abstracts of Wills, Administrations and Guardianships in NY State, 1787–1835 [database].

New York GenWeb, Ontario County

http://ontario.nygenweb.net

"Surrogate Court Proceedings from Newspapers" pre–1880, 1880–1905, 1906 to end.

"Transcripts from Actual Wills and Surrogate Proceedings" (selected).

Ontario County Dept. of Records, Archives, and Information Management Services

http://raims.com

Surrogate Court Records, 1789–1926, [Index].

Index to Surrogate Court Records 1927(+/–)–1965.

Sampubco

www.Sampubco.com

Ontario County wills are indexed 1795 to 1888 (in progress).

US Genweb Archives Project

www.usgwarchives.org

Includes Sampubco testator indexes and abstracts of some wills, Will Records, Intestate Letters of Administration, Letters Testamentary, Court Contests, Testators, Estate Appraisals.

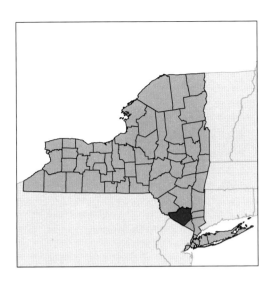

Orange County

Orange County Surrogate's Court

30 Park Place
Goshen, NY 10924

Phone   (845) 291–2193
Fax   (845) 291–2196
email   None
Hours   M–F 9:00 am to 5:00 pm
Website   www.nycourts.gov/courts/9jd/orange/surrogates.shtml

Date Formed	1 November 1683
County Seat	Goshen
Parent County	Original

Records on Microfilm at the Family History Library

Records

Wills	1787–1901
Letters Testamentary	1837–1901
Orders for proof of wills	1868–1885
Administrations	1787–1901
Letters of Administration	1787–1901
Guardianships	1823–1916
Letters of Guardianship	1823–1906
Orders Appointing Guardians	1865–1914
Orders for Special Guardians	1868–1900
Decrees	1831–1902
Orders	1858–1904
Minutes	1831–1870
Miscellaneous Orders and Decrees	1869–1901
Bonds	1890–1901
Real estate	1828–1901
Probate Packets	N/A

Indexes

Surrogates	1787–1941

Published Records and Indexes

Central New York Genealogical Society. *Tree Talks.* Syracuse, N.Y., 1961–.
❚FHL ❚NEHGS ❚NYPL ❚NYSL

Administrations	1787–1800
	32: 121–2; **33**: 119–20; **34**: 119–20; **35**: 117–8; **36**: 117–8; **37**: 115; **43**: 115–6; **45**: 111–2; **46**: 111–2
Guardianships	1802–1822
	37: 115–6; **38**: 117–8; **39**: 115–6; **40**: 115–6; **42**: 115–6; **43**: 115

Cowen, Minnie, comp. "Abstracts of Wills of Orange and Rockland Counties, New York, Volume 1" [1785–1814]. Typescript, 1937. ❚FHL ❚LOC ❚NEHGS

Heidgart, William. "Abstracts of Orange County, N.Y. Surrogate's Records — Located at Goshen, N.Y." [misc. 1829–1857] *Yesteryears: For the Appreciation and Study of New York State History* 24 (1980): 40–45. ❚FHL ❚NEHGS ❚NYPL

Surrogates Records	1829–1857

Horton, Elizabeth. "Abstract of Wills, Orange County Surrogate's Office, Goshen, New York.," *New York DAR Genealogical Records Committee Report,* 1977.

MacCormick, Elizabeth Janet. "Abstracts of Wills, Orange County, New York, 1787–1813." Typescript, 1946. ⬤FHL ❚LOC ❚NYSL

Minisink Chapter. "Abstract of Wills, Orange Count Surrogate's Office, Goshen, New York from June 27th, 1797 to December 31, 1830," *New York DAR Genealogical Records Committee Report,* series 1, volume 472 (1977). ❚DAR ❚NYPL

Orange County Genealogical Society. *Early Orange County Wills, 1731–1830.* 2 vols. Goshen, N.Y., 1991. ⬤FHL ❚NYPL

———. *Orange County Genealogical Society Quarterly.* Goshen, N.Y., 1995–. ❚FHL

Wills	1780–1805
	13: (No. 1) 6, (No. 2) 14, (No. 3) 22; **14**: (No. 1) 7, 15, (No. 3) 20, (No. 4) 30; **15**: (No. 1) 6, (No. 2) 12, (No. 3) 18; **16**: (No. 2) 12, (No. 3) 22, (No. 4) 30; **17**: (No. 1) 5, (No. 2) 14, (No. 3) 21, (No. 28); **18**: (No. 1) 5, (No. 2) 21, (No. 3) 21, (No. 4) 21; **19**: (No. 1) 21, (No. 2) 14, (No. 3) 22, (No. 4) 31; **29** (No. 1) 8–9, (No. 2) 19–20, (No. 3) 31, (No. 4) 43–45; **30**: (No. 1) 5–6, (No. 2) 19–20, (No. 3) 31, (No. 4) 40–41
Administrations	1787–1820
	13: (No. 1) 7, (No. 2) 14, (No. 3) 22; **14**: (No. 1) 7, 14, (No. 3) 20, (No. 4) 30; **15**: (No. 1) 6, (No. 2) 13, (No. 3) 18; **16**: (No. 1) 8, (No. 2) 5

Records on the Internet

New England Historic Genealogical Society
www.AmericanAncestors.org
> Abstracts of Wills, Administrations and Guardianships in NY State, 1787–1835 [database] (includes Orange County — but is incomplete some early wills and administration).

Sampubco
www.Sampubco.com
> Orange County wills from 1787 to 1857 are indexed (in progress).

US Genweb Archives Project
www.usgwarchives.org
> Includes the Sampubco Testator Indexes and abstracts of some wills

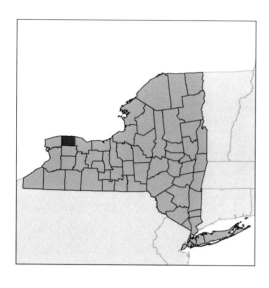

Orleans County

Orleans County Surrogate's Court

1 South Main St., Suite 3
Albion, NY 14411

Phone (585) 589–4457
Fax (585) 589–0632
email dberry@courts.state.ny.us
Hours M–F 9:00 am to 5:00 pm
Website www.nycourts.gov/courts/8jd/Orleans/index.shtml

Date Formed	11 November 1824/15 April 1825
County Seat	Albion
Parent County	Genesee

Special Notes

Some older records are on microfilm or microfiche. A few records are stored offsite. Make arrangements in advance to review records at their office.

Records on Microfilm at the Family History Library

Records		Indexes	
Wills	1825–1902	Surrogates	1825–1926
Letters	1830–1902		
Letters of Administrations	1853–1901		
Letters of Guardianships	1830–1911		
Orders	1830–1906		
Minutes	1881–1900		
Bonds	1881–1903		
Final Settlements	1854–1907		
Real Estate	1840–1900		
Probate Packets	N/A		

Published Records and Indexes

Central New York Genealogical Society. *Tree Talks*. Syracuse, N.Y., 1961–.
▮FHL ▮NEHGS ▮NYPL ▮NYSL

Records	1830–1840
Surrogate	
	6: 132
Wills	1830–1837
	9: 46, 109; **18**: 51–52, 177–8; **19**: 109; **32**: 124; **33**: 121–2;
	34: 161–2; **35**: 119–20; **36**: 119–20; **37**: 117–8; **38**: 119–20
Administrations	1825–1829, 1851–1853
	14: 96; **15**: 141–2, 221–2; **16**: 191–2; **18**: 51; **26**: 122;
	27: 121–2; **28**: 121–2; **29**: 121–2; **31**: 119
Guardianships	1842–1853
	3: 128; **4**: 42, 93, 150, 206; **5**: 33, 84, 137, 188; **6**: 38, 90;
	31: 119–20; **32**: 123–4; **38**: 120; **39**: 117–8; **40**: 117–8;
	41: 117–8; **42**: 117–8; **43**: 117–8; **44**: 115–6; **45**: 113–4;
	46: 113–4; **47**: 115–6; **48**: 111–2
Dower	1828–1851
	10: 50, 113; **22**: 121–2

Western New York Genealogical Society Journal. Hamburg, N.Y., 1974–.
▮FHL ▮NEHGS ▮NYPL ▮NYSL

Surrogate's Index	1825–1896
	30: 102–116, 152–161; **31**: 18–27, 74–84, 120–31, 173–80;
	32: 27–39, 72–84

Records on the Internet

New England Historic Genealogical Society
www.AmericanAncestors.org
 Abstracts of Wills, Administrations and Guardianships in NY State, 1787–1835 [database].

Sampubco
www.Sampubco.com
 Orange County wills from 1787 to 1857 are indexed (in progress).

US Genweb Archives Project
www.usgwarchives.org
 Includes abstracts of some wills.

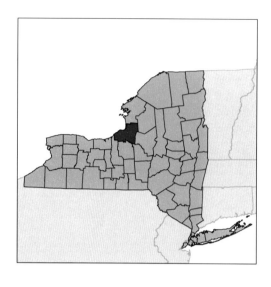

Oswego County

Oswego County Surrogate's Court

Oswego County Courthouse
25 East Oneida Street
Oswego, NY 13126

Phone	(315) 349–3295
Fax	(315) 349–8514
email	None
Hours	M–F 8:30 am to 4:30 pm
	8:30 am to 4:00 pm (summer)
Website	www.nycourts.gov/courts/5jd/oswego/index.shtml

Date Formed	1 March 1816
County Seat	Oswego
Parent County	Oneida/
	Onondaga

Records on Microfilm at the Family History Library

Records

Wills	1816–1901
Letters testamentary and of Administration	1825–1902
Letters of Administration with Will annexed	1887–1895
Order for letters of Administration	1887–1905
Administrations	1825–1904
Dower Records	1831–1880
Appointment of Guardians	1831–1852
Letters of Guardianship	1852–1894
Orders for Letters of Guardianship	1893–1809
Guardians Bonds	1890–1911

Indexes

Estates	1846–1916
General	1854–1971
Wills	1816–1915
Testamentary Index	1837–1893
Administration Index	1816–1893
Guardianship Index	1831–1916

Records (cont.)		Indexes (cont.)	
Orders Appointing			
Special Guardians	1896–1910		
Final settlements			
Guardianships	1886–1916		
Minutes of Proceedings			
& Orders, etc	1834–1865		
Common Orders	1856–1902		
Orders and decrees	1896–1904		
Surrogates Orders	1865–1896		
List of proceedings	1896–1908		
Records of appraisal	1849–1906		
Sale of real estate	1816–1860		
Bonds of Sale of Real Estate	1896–1955		
Final settlements	1856–1890		
Probate Packets	N/A	Probate Proceedings	
		Index	1896–1902

Published Records and Indexes

Central New York Genealogical Society. *Tree Talks.* Syracuse, N.Y., 1961–.
▮FHL ▮NEHGS ▮NYPL ▮NYSL

Wills	1816–1845
	6: 133, 180; **7**: 44, 99, 151; **11**: 177–8; **16**: 114, 193–4;
	17: 43–44, 105–6, 167–8; **18**: 53–54; **19**: 49; **42**: 62, 119–20,
	159–60; **43**: 61–62, 119–20, 159–60; **44**: 61–62, 117–8,
	159–60; **45**: 59–60, 115–16, 159–60; **46**: 59–60, 115–6,
	157–8; **47**: 59–60, 117–8, 159–60; **48**: 59–60, 113–4,
	159–60; **49**: 53–54
Letters of Admin	1816–1830
	49: 111–2, 159–62
Guardianships	1831–1852
	6: 39, 91, 133; **34**: 62, 121–2, 163–4; **35**: 63–64, 121–2,
	161–2; **36**: 63–64, 121–2, 161–2; **37**: 63–64, 119–20,
	163–4; **41**: 119–20
Dower:	1821–1830
	16: 113–4; **21**: 122, 175

Oswego County Genealogical Society. *Oswego Tea.* (Oswego, N.Y., 2004–2006).

Newspaper Excerpts	1815–1837
	4: (No. 3) 55–59; **6**: (No. 3) 10–11; **7**: (No. 4) 11, (No. 6) 9;
	8: (No. 1) 11, (No. 5) 10–11

Oswego County Genealogical Society Newsletter

Newspaper Excerpts	1815–1837

Samuelsen, W. David. *Oswego County, New York Will Testators Index, 1816–1901.* Salt Lake City: Sampubco, 1996. ●FHL

Records on the Internet

New England Historic Genealogical Society

www.AmericanAncestors.org

Abstracts of Wills, Administrations and Guardianships in NY State, 1787–1835 [database].

NYGenWeb, Oswego County

www.usgenweb.org

Surrogate Court Letter of Administration, 1816–1831 for Oswego Co., N.Y. "generously donated to the Oswego Co. NYGenWeb, from someone who wishes to remain anonymous."

Abstracts of select Oswego County wills.

Sampubco

www.Sampubco.com

Oswego County wills from 1816 to 1901 are indexed.

US Genweb Archives Project

www.usgwarchives.org

Includes abstracts of some wills.

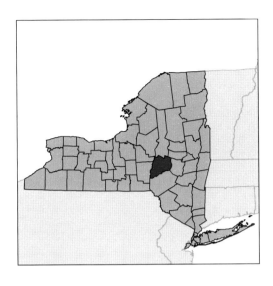

Otsego County

Otsego County Surrogate's Court

County Office Building
197 Main Street
Cooperstown, NY 13326

Date Formed	16 February 1791
County Seat	Cooperstown
Parent County	Montgomery

Phone   (607) 547–4213
Fax   (607) 547–7566
email   None
Hours   M–F 9:00 am to 5:00 pm
Website   www.nycourts.gov/courts/6jd/otsego/surrogate/index.shtml

Special Notes

Some records are stored offsite. Make arrangements in advance to review records at their office.

Records on Microfilm at the Family History Library

Records

Wills	1792–1902
Administrations	1792–1890
Letters Testamentary and of Administration	1816–1890
Administration Proceedings	1830–1886
Administrator's Bonds	1792–1864
Executors and Administrators Accounts	1827–1836
Guardianship Letters	1803–1872
Guardianship Letters, Under 14	1872–1891
Guardianship Orders Under 14	1876–1912
Guardianship Letters, Over 14	1872–1891

Indexes

Wills/Proceedings	1792–1923

Records (cont.)

Guardianship Orders, Over 14	1876–1912
Dower Book	1810–1871
Discharges	1874–1914
Final Settlement	1864–1892
Real Estate Proceedings	1813–1832
Miscellaneous records	
(Surrogates)	1781–1877
Petitions for Probate	1829–ca.1934
Probate Packets	See Petitions for Probate

Published Records and Indexes

Barber, Gertrude A., comp. *Abstracts of Wills of Otsego County, New York, 1794–1850.* 2 vols. Typescript. New York [?], 1941. ●FHL ∥NEHGS ∥NYPL

——. "Index of Wills of Otsego County, New York, from 1792–1850." Typescript. New York?, 1933. ●FHL ∥NEHGS ∥NYSL

——. "Index of Otsego County, New York, Wills, 1850–1875." Typescript. New York?, 1934. ∥LOC ∥NEHGS ∥NYSL

Central New York Genealogical Society. *Tree Talks.* Syracuse, N.Y., 1961–. ∥FHL ∥NEHGS ∥NYPL ∥NYSL

Wills	1791–1811
Administrations	1794–1822
	6: 181; **7**: 45, 100; **20**: 119–20; **21**: 51–52, 123–4; **41**: 121–2; **42**: 121–2; **43**: 121–2; **44**: 119–20; **45**: 61–62, 117–8; **46**: 61–62, 117–8; **47**: 61–62, 119–20; **48**: 61–62, 115–6; **49**: 55–56, 113–4
Guardianships	1803–1845
	22: 179–80; **23**: 177–8; **24**: 177; **25**: 179–80; **26**: 165–6; **27**: 165–6; **28**: 163–4; **29**: 165–6; **30**: 179–80; **39**: 122; **40**: 121–2
Dower	1810–1830
	7: 100, 152, 208; **8**: 42; **10**: 177; **16**: 115–6; **17**: 107–8

Records on the Internet

New England Historic Genealogical Society

www.AmericanAncestors.org

Abstracts of Wills, Administrations and Guardianships in NY State, 1787–1835 [database].

NYGenWeb, Otsego County
www.usgenweb.org
> Gertrude Barber's Abstract of Wills – 1794–1850, (see above) transcribed by Marty Irons.

> Abstracts of select Otsego County wills.

Sampubco
www.Sampubco.com
> Otsego County wills from 1791 to 1902 are indexed (in progress).

US Genweb Archives Project
www.usgwarchives.org
> Includes the Sampubco Testator Indexes (see above) and abstracts of some wills.

Putnam County

Putnam County Surrogate's Court

44 Gleneida Avenue
Carmel, NY 10512

Phone	(845) 208–7860
Fax	(845) 228–5761
email	None
Hours	M–F 9:00 am to 5:00 pm
Website	www.nycourts.gov/courts/9jd/Putnam/index.shtml

Date Formed	12 June 1812
County Seat	Carmel
Parent County	Dutchess

Records on Microfilm at the Family History Library

Records
Wills	1812–1901
Letters Testamentary	1812–1904
Letter of Administration	1812–1905
Letters of Guardianships	1812–1898
Guardian Bonds	1890–1936
Real Estate Orders	1813–1902
Probate Packets	N/A

Indexes
Surrogates	1812–1970

Published Records and Indexes

Dutchess County Genealogical Society. *The Dutchess.* (Poughkeepsie, N.Y., 1973– .
[Indexed in Periodical Source Index (PERSI) under Dutchess County—Probate
petitions at Carmel, 1809–1815.] ∎FHL ∎NEHGS ∎NYPL ∎NYSL

Probate Petitions 1812–1815
19: 67–70, 81–84

Haacker, Frederick C. "Early Settlers of Putnam County, New York." Typescript, 1946.
●FHL

MacCormick, Elizabeth Janet. *Abstract of Wills of Putnam County, N.Y.* Jackson Heights, N.Y., 1940. ▮NYPL

Records on the Internet

New England Historic Genealogical Society
www.AmericanAncestors.org

Abstracts of Wills, Administrations and Guardianships in NY State, 1787–1835 [database].

NYGenWeb, Putnam County
www.usgenweb.com

Lists Putnam County probate records abstracted in *The Dutchess*.

Sampubco
www.Sampubco.com

Putnam County wills from 1812 to 1901 are indexed (in progress).

US Genweb Archives Project
www.usgwarchives.org

Includes the Sampubco Testator Indexes and abstracts of some wills.

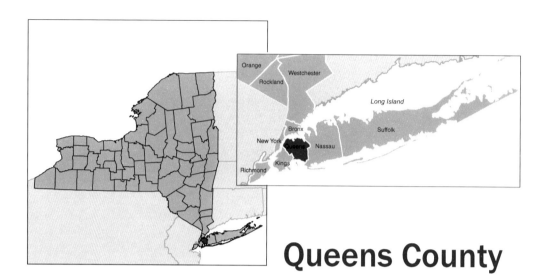

Queens County

Queens County Surrogate's Court

88–11 Sutphin Builevard, 7th Floor
Jamaica, NY 11435

Phone	(718) 298–0500
Fax	None
email	None
Hours	M–F 9:00 am to 5:00 pm
	(Record Room closed 1:00 pm to 2:00 pm)
Website	www.nycourts.gov/courts/11jd/surrogates/index.shtml

Date Formed	1 November 1683
County Seat	Jamaica
Parent County	Original

Special Notes

Card index covers estates to 1986, after which there is a computerized index. Probate files from 1962 to 1982 are on microfiche. Wills for personal estate and wills for real estate are recorded separately. Researchers are usually limited to three document requests per day.

Early Queens County wills were recorded in the deed libers. These were abstracted in the *New York Genealogical and Biographical Record* (see below).

Records on Microfilm at the Family History Library

Records		Indexes	
Card Index to Probate Records	1900–1987		
Probate Proceedings (Petitions)	1830–1865		
Wills	1787–1916	Surrogates Wills	1787–1922
Wills of real estate	1864–1916	Wills of real estate	1787–1922
Wills of personal estate	1835–1898		
Letters testamentary	1830–1916	Letters testamentary,	1830–1900

Published Records and Indexes

Abstracts of Early Wills of Queens County, New York: Recorded in Libers A and C of Deeds Now in the Registers Office at Jamaica, New York, 1683–1744. Typescript, 1940. ●FHL

Beck, Walter, and Dudley Case, comp. *Wills of Real Estate, Queens County, New York.* Typescript, 1940. ●FHL

Canfield, Amos N. "Abstracts of Early Wills of Queens Co., New York., Recorded in Libers A and C of Deeds, Now in the Register's Office at Jamaica, New York." *New York Genealogical and Biographical Record,* 1870–. Reprinted in Hoff, Henry, ed. *Long Island Source Records: from The New York Genealogical and Biographical Record.* Baltimore: Genealogical Publishing Co., 1987. ♪FHL ♪NEHGS ♪NYPL ♪NYSL

Wills	1683–1742
	65: 114–20, 245–51, 319–28.

Case, Dudley, abst. *Personal Wills, Queens County, New York, [1835–1875].* Typescript. ●FHL

———. *Wills of Real Estate, Queens County, New York.* Typescript, n.d. ●FHL

Eardeley, William A. D., comp. *Queens County, New York, Surrogate Records at Jamaica, New York, 1787–1835.* 2 vols. Typescript, n.d. ●FHL

———. *Records in the Office of the County Clerk at Jamaica, Long Island, New York, 1680–1781: Wills and Administrations, Guardians, and Inventories.* 2 vols. Brooklyn, N.Y., 1918. ●FHL

Early Wills of Riverhead, Suffolk County, New York, Sessions Book No. 1, 1669–1687: Includes Early Wills at Riverhead, Suffolk County, New York, Lester Will Book and Abstracts of Queens County Wills, Liber A of Deeds, Jamaica, Long Island, New York. Typescript. Salt Lake City, 1940. ●FHL

MacCormick, Elizabeth Janet. *Abstracts of Wills Queens County, N.Y.: 1848–1856.*

Meigs, Alice Henshaw. *Index [to] Wills of Real Estate, Queens County, New York: Libers A-G, 1787–1835.* Typescript. ●FHL ♪NYPL

Sawyer, Ray C., comp. *Abstracts of Wills for Queens County, New York, 1787–1850.* 4 vols. Typescript, 1936. ●FHL ❚NYPL

Wilson, John E. *An Index of Administrations of Queens County, New York, 1787–1908.* Typescript. ●FHL

Wilson, John E. *An Index to the Wills of Queens County, New York, 1787–1906.* Typescript. ●FHL

Records on the Internet

Sampubco
www.Sampubco.com
> Queens County wills from 1787 to 1816 are indexed (in progress).

US Genweb Archives Project
www.usgwarchives.org
> Includes the Sampubco Indexes to 1805 and abstracts of some Queens County wills filed in New York County prior to 1787.

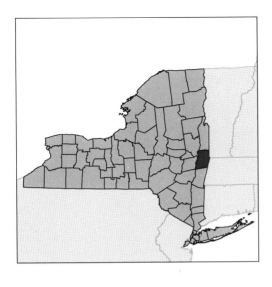

Rensselaer County

Rensselaer County Surrogate's Court

80 Second Street
Troy, NY 12180

Phone	(518) 285–6105
Fax	(518) 272–5452
email	None
Hours	M–F 9:00 am to 5:00 pm
Website	www.nycourts.gov/courts/3jd/surrogates/rensselaer/index.shtml

Date Formed	7 February 1791
County Seat	Troy
Parent County	Albany

Records on Microfilm at the Family History Library

Records		Indexes	
Wills	1791–1921	Surrogates	1794–1916
Probate Records	1792–1921		
Probate Packets	1794–20th Century		

Note: A variety of probate records are covered under the "Probate Records 1792–1901" entry in the FHLC (wills, proofs of wills, notice to creditors, final settlements, letters testamentary, letters of administration, appointments of of guardians, appointments of appraisers, bonds, transfer taxes, miscellaneous orders and decrees, order will to probate, order letters testamentary, order letters administration, order appraisers, etc.) but the FHLC does not separate them by category. Use the Surrogate's Index to find the estate and records pertaining to it.

Published Records and Indexes

Central New York Genealogical Society. *Tree Talks.* Syracuse, N.Y., 1961–.
∎FHL ∎NEHGS ∎NYPL ∎NYSL

Wills	1790–1822
	6: 182; **44**: 161–2; **45**: 119–20, 161–2; **46**: 119–20, 159–60; **47**: 161–2; **48**: 117–8, 161–2; **49**: 115–6, 163

Wills and Letters of
Admin and Test   1802–1807
                49: 164

Phillips, Ralph David. "Abstracts of All Wills, 1791 to 1821 Inclusive, Probated in Rensselaer County, New York, Formerly a Good Part of the Manor of Rensselaerwyck, Nassau, Rensselaer County, New York." 3 vols. [Vol. 2, 1818–1826; Vol. 3, 1836–1850]. Typescript, 1938. ●FHL ∥NEHGS ∥NYPL ∥NYSL

———. *Wills of Rensselaer County, New York, Abstracts of all Wills, 1794–1850.* 3 vols. Typescript. ●FHL

Shepard, Charles. "Abstracts of Wills Proved in the Court of Common Pleas of Rensselaer County, New York, from 1794 to 1822, Together with One Will from Washington County, New York." Typescript. Troy, N.Y., 1921. ●FHL ∥LOC ∥NEHGS

Wells, Maryellen. *List of Surnames Appearing in the General Index to the Rensselaer County, New York, Surrogate Records, 1794–1873: Including a Statistical Reference Map of Rensselaer County (in Centerfold) and Some Non–white Population Statistics.* Averill Park, N.Y.: Clover Homestead Publications, 1994. ∥FHL

Yearbook of the Genealogical Forum of Portland Oregon ∥FHL ∥NEHGS ∥NYPL
    Wills (misc.)   1792–1819, 1831–32, 1839–60
                7 (No. 1) 7, (No. 2) 15, (No. 3) 25, (No. 4) 33

Records on the Internet

New England Historic Genealogical Society
www.AmericanAncestors.org
    Abstracts of Wills, Administrations and Guardianships in NY State, 1787–1835 [database].

NYGenWeb, Rensselaer County
www.usgenweb.org
    Abstracts of select Rensselaer County wills.

Sampubco
www.Sampubco.com
    Rensselaer County wills from 1791 to 1875 are indexed (in progress).

US Genweb Archives Project
www.usgwarchives.org
    Includes the Sampubco Testator Indexes and abstracts of some wills.

Richmond County

Richmond County Surrogate's Court

18 Richmond Terrace
Staten Island, NY 10301–1935

Date Formed	1 November 1683
County Seat	St. George
Parent County	Original

Phone   (718) 675–8500
Fax   (718) 390–8741
email   None
Hours   M–F 9:00 am to 5:00 pm
Website   www.nycourts.gov/courts/13jd/surrogates/index.shtml

---

Records on Microfilm at the Family History Library

Records		Indexes	
Wills	1787–1967	Wills	1787–1959
Administrations	1882–1961		
Decrees on Administrations	1882–1961		
Guardianships	1787–1960		
Decrees—Guardianship	1882–1960		
Special Guardians	1882–1940		
Guardians Accounts	1919–1940		
Final Decrees	1882–1966		
Misc. Orders	1882–1967		
Probate Packets	N/A		

Published Records and Indexes

Dickinsen, Richard B. "State Island Colonial Slaves in Wills and Manumissions of Richmond Couty, New York." *Journal of the Afro-American Historical and Genealogical Society* 23 (2004): 76–90. ∎FHL

Fast, Frances S. *Court Records of Richmond County, New York, [1787–1866].* 3 vols. Typescript, 1941–1958. ●FHL ∎NYPL

Historical Records Survey (New York City). *Transcriptions of Early Town Records of New York: The Earliest Volume of Staten Island Records, 1678–1813*. New York, 1942. ●FHL

Hix, Charlotte Megill. *Staten Island Wills and Letters of Administration: Richmond County, New York, 1670–1800 as found in the Surrogate's Court, New York County, New York and abstracted by the New York Historical Society, 1892–1908, and the Staten Island references found in the New Jersey colonial documents.* Bowie, Md: Heritage Books, 1993. ∥FHL ∥NEHGS ∥NYPL

Miscellaneous Genealogical Records, Wills, Deeds, etc., 1649–1925. Typescript. ●FHL

Smith, E. Dale Hastin. *Records of Wills, Surrogates Court, Staten Island, New York (Richmond County): A Continuing Series Beginning 1787* (Spokane, Wash.: E.D.H. Smith, 1991). [Contains Will Book A, 1787–1813, Wills no. 1–50. Author did not continue series.] ∥FHL

Records on the Internet

New England Historic Genealogical Society
www.AmericanAncestors.org
Abstracts of Wills, Administrations and Guardianships in NY State, 1787–1835 [database].

Sampubco
www.Sampubco.com
Richmond County wills from 1787 to 1863 are indexed (in progress).

US Genweb Archives Project
www.usgwarchives.org
Includes the Sampubco Indexes from 1787 to 1847 and abstracts of some wills.

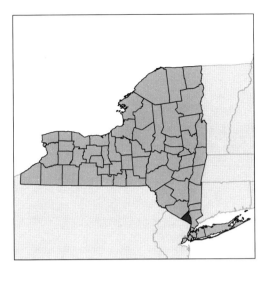

Rockland County

Rockland County Surrogate's Court

1 South Main Street, 2nd floor
New City, NY 10956

Phone	(845) 638–5330
Fax	(845) 638–5632
email	None
Hours	M–F 9:00 am to 5:00 pm
Website	www.nycourts.gov/courts/9jd/Rockland/index.shtml

Date Formed	23 February 1798
County Seat	New City
Parent County	Orange

Rockland County Archives

Building S, 40 Sanatoreum Road
Pomona, NY 10970

Phone	(845) 364–3670
Fax	(845) 364–3671
email	scheibnp@co.rockland.ny.us
Hours	M–F 9:00 am to 5:00 pm
Website	www.rocklandcountyclerk.com/archives.html

Special Notes

Original estate papers from 1798 to 1940 have been transferred to the Rockland County Archives.

Records on Microfilm at the Family History Library

Records		Indexes	
Wills, orders	1798–1901	Surrogates	1798–1901

Records (cont.)

Orange County Wills	
Transcribed	1785–1797[4]
Letters Testamentary	1798–1904
Administrations	1800–1900
Letters of Administration	1798–1900
Administrators Bonds	1890–1902
Guardianships	1805–1900
Letters Guardianship	1798–1909
Guardian Bonds	1890–1910
Dower Records	1834–1854
Minutes	1798–1901
Orders	
Decrees	1830–1900
Real estate	1802–1898
Probate Records, Proved	1802–1900
Probate Packets	1802–1900

Published Records and Indexes

Barber, Gertrude A. *Abstracts of Wills, Rockland County, New York, Book "E–H", from May 6, 1845–December 24, 1870.* 4 vols. in 2. Typescript. New York [?], 1950– 1953. ●FHL ∎NYPL ∎NYSL

———. "Index of Wills, Rockland County, New York, 1786–1845." Typescript. ●FHL ∎NEHGS

Cowen, Minnie, comp. "Abstracts of Wills of Orange and Rockland Counties, New York, 1770–1845." 3 vols. [Vol. 1, 1785–1816; Vol. 2, 1816–1833; Vol. 3, 1833– 1850]. Typescript, 1937, 1939. ●FHL ∎LOC ∎NEHGS ∎NYSL

———. *Abstracts of Wills of Rockland County, New York, 1786–1845.* New York, 1937–1939.

Genealogical Society of Rockland County. *Genealogical Society of Rockland County Newsletter* (New City, N.Y., 1986–). ∎FHL ∎NEHGS

Dower	1833–1854
	7: (No. 3) 4–5
Slaves in Wills	1700s+
	12: (No. 3) 4–6

---

[4] Rockland County was created from Orange County in 1798, and this copy of wills was transcribed in 1855.

Records on the Internet

New England Historic Genealogical Society

www.AmericanAncestors.org

Abstracts of Wills, Administrations and Guardianships in NY State, 1787–1835 [database].

Sampubco

www.Sampubco.com

Rockland County wills from 1798 to 1901 are indexed 1798 to 1901.

US Genweb Archives Project

www.usgwarchives.org

Includes the Sampubco Testator Indexes and abstracts of some wills.

Saint Lawrence County

**St. Lawrence County
Surrogate's Court**
48 Court Street
Canton, NY 13617–1194

Phone	(315) 379–2217
Fax	(315) 379–2372
email	None
Hours	M–F 9:00 am to 5:00 pm
	M–F 8:00 am to 4:00 pm (summer)
Website	www.nycourts.gov/courts/4jd/stlawrence/surrogates.shtml

Date Formed	3 March 1802
County Seat	Canton
Parent County	Clinton, Herkimer, and Montgomery

Records on Microfilm at the Family History Library

Records

Wills	1830–1916
Administrations	1831–1917
Letters Testamentary & of Admininstration	1831–1917
Letters of Guardianship	1830–1927
Dower Records	1830–1871
Minutes & Orders	1830–1919
Real Estate Sales	1842–1904[5]
Bonds	1890–1915
Probate Packets	N/A

Indexes

Wills & Proceedings	1830–1955
Index to Administration of Intestate Estates	1830–1955

---

[5] Real estate sales before 1842 are recorded in the first volume of minutes and orders

Published Records and Indexes

Central New York Genealogical Society. *Tree Talks.* Syracuse, N.Y., 1961–.
*I*FHL *I*NEHGS *I*NYPL *I*NYSL

Wills	1823–1829
	6: 43, 94, 136, 184; **7**: 45, 103, 107, 155, 164, 224; **9**: 51; **24**: 59
Administrations	1808–1828
Guardianships	1810–1820
Dowers:	1810–1820

Misc. (admin, dower, guard., mixed together)
    22: 55–56, 183–4; **23**: 55–56; **24**: 55–56; **25**: 57–58; **26**: 169; **38**: 125–6, 165–6; **39**: 123–4, 163–4; **40**: 123–4, 163–4; **41**: 123; **45**: 121–2, 163–4; **46**: 121–2

Letters Test. & Admin: 1831–1841
    41: 123–4, 163–4; **42**: 123–4, 163–4; **43**: 123–4, 163–4; **44**: 123–4, 163–4; **45**: 121

Samuelsen, W. David. *St. Lawrence County, New York, Will Testators Index, 1830–1916.* Salt Lake City: Sampubco, 1995. ●FHL

Records on the Internet

New England Historic Genealogical Society
www.AmericanAncestors.org
    Abstracts of Wills, Administrations and Guardianships in NY State, 1787–1835 [database].

Sampubco
www.Sampubco.com
    St. Lawrence County wills from 1830 to 1916 are indexed.

US Genweb Archives Project
www.usgwarchives.org
    Includes abstracts of some wills.

Saratoga County

Saratoga County Surrogate's Court

Municipal Center
30 McMaster Street
Ballston Spa, NY 12020

Date Formed   7 February 1791
County Seat   Ballston Spa
Parent County Albany

Phone   (518) 451–8830
Fax   (518) 884–4774
email   None
Hours   M–F 9:00 am to 5:00 pm
Website   www.nycourts.gov/courts/4jd/saratoga/index.shtml

Special Notes

The surrogate's office has a card file for all estates.

Records on Microfilm at the Family History Library

Records		Indexes	
Wills	1791–1921	Surrogates	1799–1904
Letters Testamentary	1829–1918		
Orders of Wills	1857–1895		
Letters of Administrations	1815–1929		
Administration Bonds	1890–1904		
Orders of Administration	1857–1882		
Letter of Guardianships	1815–1915		
Orders of Guardianships	1857–1909		
Guardian Bonds	1890–1902		
Dower Records	1833–1866		
Minutes	1832–1881		
Decrees	1883–1902		
Probate Packets	N/A		

Published Records and Indexes

Central New York Genealogical Society. *Tree Talks.* Syracuse, N.Y., 1961–.
▮FHL ▮NEHGS ▮NYPL ▮NYSL

Administrations	1815–1847	
	5: 37, 88, 141, 192; **6**: 42; **26**: 171–2; **27**: 171–2; **28**: 169–70;	
	29: 171; **33**: 171–2; **34**: 171–2; **35**: 167–8; **36**: 167–8;	
	37: 167–8; **38**: 167–8; **39**: 165–6; **40**: 165–6; **41**: 165–6;	
	42: 165–6; **43**: 165–6; **44**: 165–6; **45**: 165–6; **46**: 163–4;	
	47: 165–6; **48**: 165–6	
Record of Wills	1806–1812	
	49: 119–20, 167–8	
Guardianship		
	2: 55, 79; **3**: 23, 59, 96; **19**: 55; **25**: 60, 183–4	
Surrogates		
	6: 93, 135, 183; **7**: 47, 102, 154, 210; **8**: 44	

Durkee, Cornelius E., comp. "Abstract of Surrogate Records in Saratoga County, [New York], 1791–1806." Typescript. Saratoga Springs, N.Y., 1876–1877. ●FHL

Ellsberry, Elizabeth Prather, comp. *Will Records of Saratoga County, New York, 1796–1805.* Chillicothe, Mo.: E. P. Ellsberry, 1973?. ●FHL

MacCormick, Elizabeth Janet. *Abstracts of Wills, Saratoga County, New York, 1791–1815.* Typescript, 1938. ●FHL ▮LOC ▮NYPL

Samuelsen, W. David. *Saratoga County, New York, Will Testators Index, 1799–1920.* Salt Lake City: Sampubco, 1992.

―――. *Saratoga County, New York, 1799–1921 Index to Willbooks.* Salt Lake City: Sampubco, 1992. ▮NYPL

The Saratoga. Rhinebeck, N.Y.: Kinship, 1984–1998. ▮FHL ▮NEHGS ▮NYPL

Wills	1791–1805	
	1: 128; **2**: 32–34, 51–55, 91–93, 127–28; **3**: 14–16, 62–63.	
Letters of Admin.	1791–1806	
	1: 119–21; **2**: 20–22, 65	
	1815–1826	
	1: 18–21, 58–59, 83–84, 119; **2**: 65–66 [last entry indicates "to be continued," but it was never brought any further forward]	

Records on the Internet

New England Historic Genealogical Society

www.AmericanAncestors.org

Abstracts of Wills, Administrations and Guardianships in NY State, 1787–1835 [database].

Sampubco

www.Sampubco.com

Saratoga County wills from 1791 to 1921 are indexed.

US Genweb Archives Project

www.usgwarchives.org

Includes abstracts of some wills.

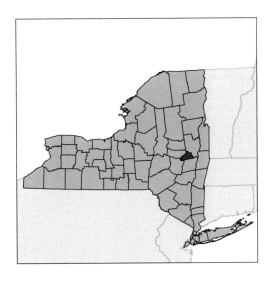

Schenectady County

Schenectady County Surrogate's Court

612 State Street
Schenectady, NY 12305–2113

Phone	(518) 285–8455
Fax	(518) 377–6378
email	None
Hours	M–F 9:00 am to 5:00 pm
	M–F 8:30 am to 4:30 pm (summer)
Website	www.nycourts.gov/courts/4jd/schenectady/index.shtml

Date Formed	7 March 1809
County Seat	Schenectady
Parent County	Albany

Special Notes

All records are onsite. Some of the older probate files are available for research on microfilm only.

Records on Microfilm at the Family History Library

Records		Indexes	
Wills	1806–1917	Surrogates	1809–1916
Letters Testamentary	1809–1918		
Probate of Wills	1871–1917		
Letters of Administrations	1809–1921		
Administration Bonds	1890–1901		
Letters of Guardianship	1809–1907		
Guardian's Bonds	1890–1929		
Real estate–dower	1817–1863		
Dower Records	1817–1858		
Minutes of Proceedings	1830–1857		
Probate of Wills	1871–1917		
Probate Packets	N/A		

Published Records and Indexes

Barber, Gertrude A., comp. "Abstracts of Wills of Schenectady County, New York, Copied from the Original Records at the Suffogate's Office, Schenectady, N.Y." 3 vol. [vol. 1, 1809–1820; vol. 2, 1820–1835; vol. 3, 1836–1845]. Typescript. [New York?], 1941. ●FHL ▮NEHGS

―――. *Abstracts of Wills of Schenectady County, New York, 1820–1845.* Vols. 2–3. Typescript. New York [?], n.d. ●FHL ▮NYPL

―――. *Abstracts of Wills of Schenectady County, New York: Copied from the Original Records at the Court House, Schenectady, New York.* 3 vols. Typescript. New York [?], 1943[?]. ●FHL ▮LOC ▮NEHGS ▮NYPL ▮NYSL

―――. *Abstracts of Wills of Schenectady County, N.Y.* 1941.

Central New York Genealogical Society. *Tree Talks.* Syracuse, N.Y., 1961–. ▮FHL ▮NEHGS ▮NYPL ▮NYSL

Wills	1804–1830, 1877–1881
	7: 48; **26**: 174; **31**: 173–4; **32**: 173–4; **33**: 173–4; **34**: 173–4;
	35: 169–70; **36**: 169–70; **37**: 169–70; **38**: 169–70;
	39: 167–8; **40**: 167–8; **41**: 167–8; **42**: 167–8; **43**: 167–8;
	44: 167; **47**: 167–8; **48**: 167–8; **49**: 169–70
Administrations	1809–1850
	44: 168; **45**: 167–8; **46**: 165–6; **47**: 167
Guardianships	1809–1858
Dower	1717–1835
	16: 196; **17**: 175–6; **18**: 55–56; **25**: 186; **26**: 173–4

The Mohawk. Rhinebeck, N.Y.: Kinship, 1984–1998. ▮FHL ▮NEHGS ▮NYPL

Letters of Admin.	1809–1850
	1: 33–34, 56–57, 87–88, 130–131; **2**: 31–32, 61–63
Book of Guardians	1809–1858
	1: 8–9, 54–55, 80, 119–20; **2**: 23, 53–55

Samuelsen, W. David. *Schenectady County, New York Wills, 1809–1845.* Salt Lake City: Samuelsen Pub., 1991. ▮NYPL

Records on the Internet

New England Historic Genealogical Society

www.AmericanAncestors.org

Abstracts of Wills, Administrations and Guardianships in NY State, 1787–1835 [database].

NYGenWeb, Schenectady County

www.usgenweb.org

Contains direct links to the will abstracts at the US Genweb Archives Project.

Sampubco

www.Sampubco.com

Schenectady County wills from 1809 to 1917 are indexed.

US Genweb Archives Project

www.usgwarchives.org

Includes abstracts of some wills.

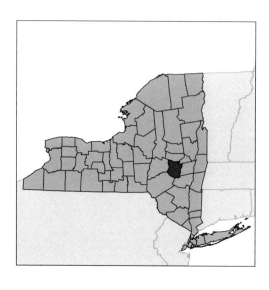

Schoharie County

Schoharie County Surrogate's Court
290 Main Street
Schoharie, NY 12157

Mailing Address
PO Box 669
Schoharie, NY 12157

Phone	(518) 295–8387
Fax	(518) 295–8451
email	None
Hours	M–F 9:00 am to 5:00 pm
Website	www.nycourts.gov/courts/3jd/surrogates/schoharie/index.shtml

Date Formed	6 April 1795/ 1 Jun 1795
County Seat	Schoharie
Parent County	Albany

Records on Microfilm at the Family History Library

Records

Wills	1795–1913
Letters, Testamentary & of Administration	1812–1881
Letters, Testamentary	1882–1898
Letters Testamentary	1897–1911
Letters, Administration	1881–1910
Administrator Bonds	1890–1904
Guardian Records	1830–1881
General Guardians	1882–1901
Guardian bonds	1890–1913
Orders; guard., admin.,	1872–1933
Dower Records	1817–1863
Minutes & Orders	1830–1904
Final Settlements	1873–1901
Probate of Wills	1872–1891

Indexes

Surrogates	1795–1902

Records (cont.)

Orders, Probate of Wills	1873–1907
Common orders	1872–1904
Probate Packets	N/A

Published Records and Indexes

Barber, Gertrude A., comp. *Abstracts of Wills, Letters of Administration, Letters of Guardianship, of Schoharie County, New York, 1795–1863.* 5 vols. Typescript. New York [?], 1938. ●FHL ▮LOC ▮NEHGS ▮NYPL ▮NYSL

Central New York Genealogical Society. *Tree Talks.* Syracuse, N.Y., 1961–).
▮FHL ▮NEHGS ▮NYPL

Wills	1787–1813, 1823–1829
	8: 109, 165, 225; **10**: 181, 269–70; **13**: 177; **16**: 197–8;
	17: 177–8; **18**: 121–2; **23**: 185–6; **24**: 185–6; **26**: 175–6;
	27: 173–4; **28**: 171; **32**: 175–6; **33**: 175–6; **34**: 175–6;
	35: 171–2; **36**: 171–2; **37**: 171–2; **38**: 171–2; **39**: 169–70;
	40: 169–70; **41**: 169–70; **42**: 169–70; **43**: 169–70;
	44: 169–70; **45**: 169–70; **46**: 167–8; **47**: 169–70; **48**: 169–70; **49**: 171–2

Records on the Internet

New England Historic Genealogical Society
www.AmericanAncestors.org
Abstracts of Wills, Administrations and Guardianships in NY State, 1787–1835 [database].

NYGenWeb, Schoharie County
www.usgenweb.org
"Index to Letters of Testamentary Administration 1860–1871 Schoharie County, NY," transcribed by Angeles Oakes.
Abstracts of select Schoharie County wills.

Sampubco
www.Sampubco.com
Schoharie County wills from 1795 to 1903 are indexed.

US Genweb Archives Project
www.usgwarchives.org
Includes abstracts of some wills.

Schuyler County

Schuyler County Surrogate's Court

105 Ninth Street, Unit 35
Watkins Glen, NY 14891

Phone   (607) 535–7144
Fax   (607) 535–4918
email   None
Hours   9:00 am to 5:00 pm
Website www.nycourts.gov/courts/6jd/schuyler/surrogate/index.shtml

Date Formed	17 April 1854
County Seat	Watkins Glen
Parent County	Chemung/ Steuben/Tompkins

Records on Microfilm at the Family History Library

Records		Indexes	
Wills	1854–1901	Surrogates	1855–1970
Wills, (transcribed from Tompkins, Steuben, Chemung Cos)	1829–1861		
Letters Testamentary	1855–1903		
Letters of Administration	1859–1903		
Administration Bonds	1874–1910		
Letters of Guardianship	1855–1905		
Dower Records	1859–1880		
Minutes & Orders	1860–1871		
Minutes, Orders, & Decrees	1879–1907		
Final settlements	1858–1898		
Judical Settlements	1880–1917		
Real Estate	1895–1916		
Probate Packets	N/A		

Published Records and Indexes

Central New York Genealogical Society. *Tree Talks.* Syracuse, N.Y., 1961–.
▮FHL **▮**NEHGS **▮**NYPL **▮**NYSL

Wills	1855–1860
	19: 185–6; **23**: 59–60; **30**: 123–4, 181; **38**: 174; **39**: 171–2;
	44: 171–2; **45**: 171–2; **46**: 169–70; **47**: 171–2; **48**: 171–2;
	49: 173–4
Guardianships	1855–1866
	30: 182; **31**: 177–8; **32**: 177–8; **34**: 63–64; **35**: 173–4;
	40: 171–2; **41**: 171–2; **42**: 171–2; **43**: 171–2; **44**: 171
Dower:	1858–1880
	19: 57–58, 185

Records on the Internet

NYGenWeb, Schuyler County
www.usgenweb.org
   Abstracts of select Schuyler County wills and guardianships.

Sampubco
www.Sampubco.com
   Schuyler County wills from 1854 to 1861 are indexed.

US Genweb Archives Project
www.usgwarchives.org
   Includes abstracts of some wills.

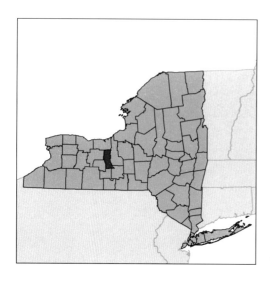

Seneca County

Seneca County Surrogate's Court

48 W. Williams St.
Waterloo, NY 13165

Phone	(315) 539–7531
Fax	(315) 539–3267
email	rcapozzi@courts.state.ny.us
Hours	M–F 9:00 am to 5:00 pm
Website	www.nycourts.gov/courts/7jd/courts/surrogates

Date Formed	24 March 1804
County Seat	Waterloo, Ovid
Parent County	Cayuga

Records on Microfilm at the Family History Library

Records

Wills	1804–1919
Administrations	1815–1900
Letters Testamentary, & of Administration	1827–1900
Letters of Guardianship	1816–1901
Admeasurement of Dower	1829–1876
Minutes, Orders, Decrees	1830–1903
Bonds	1890–1903
Journals	1847–1918
Judicial settlements	1854–1902
Probate Packets	N/A

Indexes

Surrogates	1804–1914

Published Records and Indexes

Central New York Genealogical Society. *Tree Talks.* Syracuse, N.Y., 1961–.
▮FHL ▮NEHGS ▮NYPL ▮NYSL

Guardianship

8: 166, 226; **9**: 53, 116, 181

Dower

12: 223–4; **13**: 104–5; **14**: 105

Estate Records

4: 48, 99, 156, 213; **5**: 144, 196

Wills and Admin

6: 45, 96, 138, 187; **7**: 49, 104, 157, 212; **8**: 47, 110, 166;
11: 110, 229; **14**: 105–6; **15**: 71–72, 153; **27**: 177–8; **28**: 175;
32: 180; **33**: 177–8; **34**: 177–8; **35**: 127, 128

Reynolds, Stanley I., comp. "Collection of Seneca County [New York] Wills, Petitions for Probate, and Guardianships." Typescript. ●FHL

Records on the Internet

New England Historic Genealogical Society
www.AmericanAncestors.org
Abstracts of Wills, Administrations and Guardianships in NY State, 1787–1835 [database].

NYGenWeb, Seneca County
www.usgenweb.org
Abstracts of select Seneca County wills and guardianships.

Sampubco
www.Sampubco.com
Seneca County wills from 1804 to 1904 are indexed.

US Genweb Archives Project
www.usgwarchives.org
Includes abstracts of some wills.

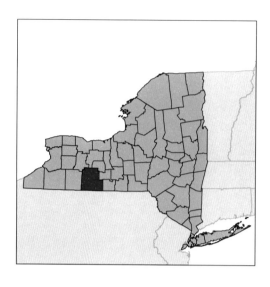

Steuben County

Steuben County Surrogate's Court

3 East Pulteney Square
Bath, NY 14810

Phone   (607) 776–7126
Fax   (607) 776–4987
email   pplanke@courts.state.ny.us
Hours   M–F 9:00 am to 5:00 pm
Website www.nycourts.gov/courts/7jd/courts/surrogates

Date Formed	18 March 1796
County Seat	Bath
Parent County	Ontario

Records on Microfilm at the Family History Library

Records

Wills	1800–1869
Letters Testamentary	1861–1872
Administrations	1822–1870
Letters of Administration	1860–1870
Guardianships	1828–1873
Orders appointing Special guardians	1830–1866
Dower Records	1829–1876
Minutes & Orders	1840–1881
Minutes, Orders	1853–1858
Minutes, Orders, & Decrees	1830–1881
Orders; Testamentary, and Administration	1855–1860
Orders of Administration	1861–1870
Orders; Testamentary	1861–1870
Accounts of Executors and Administrators	1830–1857

Indexes

Testamentary	1796–1936
Administration	1796–1936
Guardian	1796–1909

Records (cont.)

Sales of Real Estate	1828–1867
Final Settlements	1854–1868
Probate Packets	N/A

Published Records and Indexes

Central New York Genealogical Society. *Tree Talks.* Syracuse, N.Y., 1961–.
    ∎FHL ∎NEHGS ∎NYPL ∎NYSL

Wills	1800–1813
	34: 179–80; **35**: 177–8; **45**: 175–6; **46**: 173–4; **47**: 123–4, 175–6; **48**: 123–4, 175–6; **49**: 123–4, 177–8
Administrations	1825–1828, 1847–1852, 1822–1847
	37: 177–8; **38**: 177–8
Guardianships	1814–1829
	19: 187–8; **20**: 125–6, 185–6
Dower:	1828–1848, 1861–1881
	21: 61–62; **23**: 188; **24**: 123–4
Letters Test. & Admin.	1847–1851
	38: 178; **39**: 175–6; **40**: 175–6; **41**: 175–6; **42**: 175–6; **43**: 175–6; **44**: 175–6; **45**: 175

Records on the Internet

New England Historic Genealogical Society
www.AmericanAncestors.org
    Abstracts of Wills, Administrations and Guardianships in NY State, 1787–1835 [database].

Sampubco
www.Sampubco.com
    Steuben County wills from 1800 to 1869 are indexed.

US Genweb Archives Project
www.usgwarchives.org
    Includes abstracts of some wills.

Suffolk County

Suffolk County Surrogate's Court

County Center Building
320 Center Drive
Riverhead, NY 11901

Date Formed	1 Nov 1683
County Seat	Riverhead
Parent County	Original

Phone   (631) 852-1745 (General)
               (631) 852-1724 (Records)
email
Hours   M-F 9:00 am to 5:00 pm
Website   www.nycourts.gov/courts/10jd/suffolk/surrogates.shtml

Special Notes

Many original records and microform files are available on-site, but others are archived in a nearby storage facility. Requested items from that facility are retrieved twice a day: at 10 am and 2 pm. Files from 1988 and later are indexed on computers available for public use. The court has begun to digitize the index to pre-1988 files from the existing card index. The conversion is proceeding alphabetically, not chronologically.

Early Suffolk County wills can be found in a number of places. See Diane F. Perry, "Suffolk County Wills Where Are They?" in *Suffolk County Historical Register* 3(1978): 66–69.

Records on Microfilm at the Family History Library:

Records	Indexes
None	None

Published Records and Indexes

"Contents of Session Book, Riverhead, Suffolk County, Long Island, New York, 1669–1684." Typescript. ●FHL

Cooper, Thomas W. *The Records of the Court of Sessions of Suffolk County in the Province of New York, 1670–1688.* Bowie, Md.: Heritage Books, 1993.

Eardeley, William A. D. "Suffolk County, New York: Surrogate Records at Riverhead, New York, 1787–1829: Indexes of Wills and Abstracts." 2 vols. Typescript. ●FHL ◢LOC

Easter, George M., abst. The Wills of Suffolk County on Long Island in the State of New York: Liber A, 1787–1798. 1937. ●FHL Also published in book form in 2001 and 2007 by Heritage Books, Westminster, Maryland. ◢LOC ◢NYSL

Kerr, John C. "Some Suffolk County, Long Island, Wills of Brush, Gildersleeve, and Dennis Families, Recorded at Greenport, Long Island, 1786–1819." Typescript. ●FHL

Pelletreau, William S. *Early Long Island Wills of Suffolk County, 1691–1703: An Unabridged Copy of the Manuscript Volume Known as "The Lester Will Book", Being the Record of the Prerogative Court of the County of Suffolk, New York; with Genealogical and Historical Notes.* New York: F. P. Harper, 1897. ●FHL ◢LOC

Petty, Joseph H. "Abstracts of Brookhaven, (L.I.) Wills, On Record in the Surrogate's Office at New York" *The New York Genealogical and Biographical Record* 9 (1880): 24–29; 12 (1881): 46–49, 198–9; 14 (1883): 140–2; 24 (1893): 88–90, 142–4.

Van Buren, Elizabeth R. "Abstracts of Intestate Records of Suffolk County." 2 vols. Typescript. 1931. ●FHL

———— "Abstracts of Wills, Recorded at Riverhead, Suffolk County, New York." 9 vols. in 6. Typescript. 1931–1932. ●FHL

————. "Probate Records of Suffolk County Recorded at Riverhead, New York, 1780–1849." 13 vols. Typescript. ●FHL

Records on the Internet

New England Historic Genealogical Society
www.AmericanAncestors.org
> Abstracts of Wills, Administrations and Guardianships in NY State, 1787–1835 [database].

New York GenWeb, Suffolk County
www.usgenweb.org
> Has user-submitted abstracts of wills arranged by family name. Also many pre-1787 wills probated in New York County.

US Genweb Archives Project
www.usgwarchives.org/ny
> Includes of abstracts of pre-1787 Wills and Letters of Administration

Sullivan County

Sullivan County Surrogate's Court
Sullivan County Government Center
100 North St., Room 250
PO Box 5012
Monticello, NY 12701

Date Formed	27 March 1809
County Seat	Monticello
Parent County	Ulster

Phone   (845) 807–0690
Fax   (845) 794–0310
email   lhering@courts.state.ny.us
Hours   M–F 9:00 am to 5:00 pm
Website   www.nycourts.gov/courts/3jd/surrogates/sullivan/index.shtml

Special Notes
Nearly all existing records lost in a fire in 1909.

Records on Microfilm at the Family History Library
None

Published Records and Indexes

Barber, Gertrude A. *Index to Proceedings in Administration of Intestates Estates, at the Surrogates Office, Monticello, Sullivan County, N.Y.* 1949.

———. *Index of Wills, Sullivan County, New York, 1876–1909.* Typescript. New York [?], 1950. ●FHL ∎NYPL

———. *Index of Wills of Sullivan County, New York this Index includes the Records of all Wills Admitted to Probate from April, 1876, to the date of the fire, August 10, 1909 being Liber of Wills 8 to 16, inclusive also the Wills Recorded pursuant to Chapter 219 of the Laws of 1910 in Book of Wills Number One Will Records One to Seven, Inclusive, were Burned on August 10, 1909.* 1900; reprint, Ann Arbor, Michigan University Microfilms International – Books on Demand, 1990. ∎NYPL ∎NYSL

Records on the Internet

New England Historic Genealogical Society
www.AmericanAncestors.org
> Abstracts of Wills, Administrations and Guardianships in NY State, 1787–1835 [database].(Includes Sullivan County because Eardeley made his abstracts prior to the fire. This is an invaluable resource. Some of Eardeley's abstracts date from as late as the 1840s.)

US Genweb Archives Project
www.usgwarchives.org
> Includes abstracts of two Sullivan County wills filed in other counties.

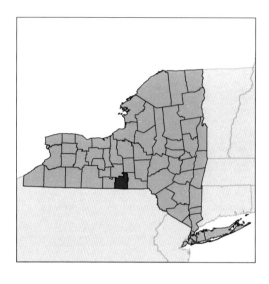

Tioga County

Tioga County Surrogate's Court
Court Annex Building
20 Court St.
Owego, NY 13827

Date Formed	16 February 1791
County Seat	Owego
Parent County	Montgomery

Mailing Address
Courthouse
PO Box 10
Owego, NY 13827

Phone	(607) 687–1303
Fax	(607) 687–3240
email	None
Hours	M–F 9:00 am to 5:00 pm
Website	www.nycourts.gov/courts/6jd/tioga/surrogate/index.shtml

---

Special Notes

Some records are stored offsite, but are within easy walking distance of the surrogate court's office.

Records on Microfilm at the Family History Library

Records

Wills	1798–1905
Letters Testamentary	1840–1901
Administrations	1825–1847
	1873–1936
Guardian Appointment, Account	1840–1890
Letters of Guardianship	1858–1947
Letters of Administration, Wills, Accounts, Executors,	

Indexes

Surrogates	1800–1969

Records (cont.)

Administrators	1825–1847
1873–1936[6]	
Letters of Administration	
Guardianship, & Testamentary	1852–1923
Book Relative to dower v. A–B	1810–1840
Proceedings in Dower	1841–1881
Sale of Real Estate	1804–1874
Surrogate Minutes, Orders	
Decrees, etc.	1825–1835
Minutes & Order Books	1840–1909
Minutes & Orders and Decrees	1882–1969
Final Settlement	1858–1902
Probate Packets	N/A
Miscellaneous Records	
(County Clerk)	1829–1964

Published Records and Indexes

Barber, Gertrude A. *Abstracts of Wills of Tioga County, New York, at the Surrogate's Court, Owego, New York, 1799–1847.* Typescript. New York [?], n.d. ●FHL ▌NYPL

Canfield, Amos. "Abstracts of Wills Taken from the Probate Records of Tioga County, New York." New York Genealogical and Biographical Society. *New York Genealogical and Biographical Record* (New York, 1870–). ▌FHL ▌NEHGS

Wills	1798–1843
	57: 381–86; **58**: 67–76, 277–87 [last entry indicates "to be continued," but it was never brought any further forward]

Central New York Genealogical Society. *Tree Talks.* Syracuse, N.Y, 1961–.
▌FHL ▌NEHGS ▌NYPL ▌NYSL

Wills	1805–1817
	5: 42, 92, 146; **32**: 181–2; **33**: 127–8, 179–80; **34**: 123–4
Administrations	1798–1802, 1814–1818
	27: 181–2; **28**: 63–64
Guardianships	1808–1845
	46: 175–6; **47**: 177–8; **48**: 177–8; **49**: 57–58, 179–80
Dower:	1817–1837
	28: 64, 127–8
Letters Test. & Admin.	1840–1859
	40: 177–8; **41**: 177–8; **42**: 177–8; **43**: 177–8; **44**: 177–8; **45**: 177–8

Woodward, Shirley L, comp. "Records of Broome and Tioga Counties." Typescript. ●FHL

---

[6] This FHLC entry was not broken down any further.

Records on the Internet

New England Historic Genealogical Society

www.AmericanAncestors.org

Abstracts of Wills, Administrations and Guardianships in NY State, 1787–1835 [database].

Sampubco

www.Sampubco.com

Tioga County wills from 1798 to 1904 are indexed.

US Genweb Archives Project

www.usgwarchives.org

Includes abstracts of some wills.

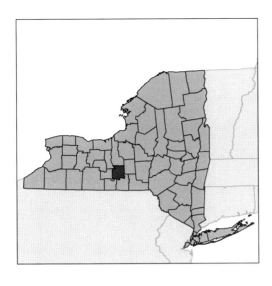

Tompkins County

Tompkins County Surrogate's Court
Tompkins County Courthouse
320 North Tioga St.
Ithaca, NY 14850

Date Formed	7 April 1817
County Seat	Ithaca
Parent County	Broome, Cayuga, and Seneca

Mailing Address
Tompkins County Surrogate's Court
320 North Tioga St
PO Box 70
Ithaca, NY 14851–0070

Phone	(607) 277–0622
Fax	(212) 457–2952
email	None
Hours	M–F 9:00 am to 5:00 pm
	(Office may close during lunch hour)
Website	www.nycourts.gov/courts/6jd/tompkins/surrogate/index.shtml

---

Records on Microfilm at the Family History Library

Records		Indexes	
Wills	1817–1903	Surrogates	1818–1910
Administrations	1823–1904	Wills & Proceedings	1910–1936
Letters of Administration,		Wills, Admin., Guard.	1936–1951
Testamentary	1823–1904		
Letters Testamentary	1881–1904		
Administrator Bonds	1890–1896		
Guardianships	1817–1916		
Special Guardian	1870–1913		
General Guardian	1853–1916		
Dower Book	1817–1882		

Records (cont.)

Petitions and Proofs	1818–1900
Minutes, Orders & Decrees	1831–1896
Admin. Minutes, Orders, & Decrees	1896–1910
Exec. Minutes, Orders, & Decrees	1862–1910
Final Settlements	1868–1907
Sale of real estate	1831–1907
Miscellaneous bonds	1896–1901
Probate Packets	See Petitions and Proofs
Miscellaneous Records (County Clerk)	1817–1905

Published Records and Indexes

Barber, Gertrude A. *Abstracts of Wills of Tompkins County, New York, 1817–1833: Copied from the Original Records at the Surrogate's Office, Ithaca, New York.* Typescript. New York [?], 1941. ●FHL ∎LOC ∎NYPL ∎NYSL

Cayuga Chapter. "Unpublished Wills of Tompkins County." *New York DAR Genealogical Records Committee Report*, series 2, volume 64 (1947). ∎DAR

Haynes, Myrte Rice. *Abstracts of Intestate Estates, Tompkins County, New York 1850–1875.* Typescript, 1966. New York Public Library. ∎NYPL

New York DAR. "Unpublished Records–Abstracts Tompkins County Estates; Records Baptist church, Clyde, Wayne Co." *New York DAR Genealogical Records Committee Report*, series 1, volume 284 (1966). ∎DAR

Central New York Genealogical Society. *Tree Talks.* Syracuse, N.Y., 1961–.
∎FHL ∎NEHGS ∎NYPL ∎NYSL

Wills	1817–1824
Administrations	1817–1858
	18: 57–58; **19**: 119–20; **20**: 63–67, 189–90; **21**: 127–8; **22**: 127–8; **31**: 183–4; **32**: 183–4; **33**: 181–2; **34**: 181–2; **35**: 181–2; **36**: 181–2
Dower	
	15: 77–78, 159–60; **16**: 51–52, 199–200; **17**: 181–2
Guardianships	1829–1839
	8: 113, 169; **29**: 184; **30**: 189–90; **31**: 183; **38**: 181–2; **39**: 179–80; **40**: 179; **41**: 180; **42**: 179–80; **43**: 179–80; **44**: 179–80; **45**: 179–80; **46**: 177–8; **47**: 179–80; **48**: 179–80; **49**: 59–60, 181–2
Miscellaneous:	Pre-1817

Records on the Internet

New England Historic Genealogical Society

www.AmericanAncestors.org

> Abstracts of Wills, Administrations and Guardianships in NY State, 1787–1835 [database].

NYGenWeb, Tompkins County

www.usgenweb.org

> Includes a full-text index to wills (also on RootsWeb.com).

Sampubco

www.Sampubco.com

> Tompkins County wills form 1817 to 1903 are indexed.

US Genweb Archives Project

www.usgwarchives.org

> Includes abstracts of some wills.

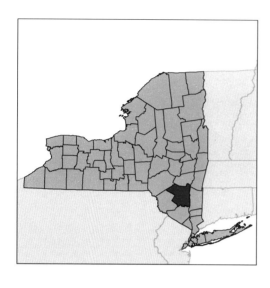

Ulster County

Ulster County Surrogate's Court
240 Fair Street, 3rd floor
Kingston, NY 12401

Mailing Address
Chief Clerk
Ulster County Surrogate's Court
PO Box 1800
Kingston, NY 12402

Phone	(845) 340–3348, (845) 340–3350
Fax	(845) 340–3352
email	None
Hours	M–F 9:00 am to 5:00 pm
Website	www.nycourts.gov/courts/3jd/surrogates/ulster/index.shtml

Date Formed	1 November 1683
County Seat	Kingston
Parent County	Original

Special Notes

All probate records are available onsite. Older records have been microfilmed, and the original files are archived offsite.

Records on Microfilm at the Family History Library

Records

Wills	1787–1917
Administrations	1787–1916
Guardian Records	1823–1919
Letters Testamentary & of Administration	1787–1861
Letters Testamentary	1862–1903

Indexes

Surrogates	1895–1959
Wills	1787–1916
Letters Administration	1787–1914

Records (cont.)

Letters Administration	1862–1916
Bonds of Administration	1890–1906
Special guardian,	
Judicial Settlement	1904–1920
Guardian Decrees	1861–1902
Minutes of Guardianship	1876–1904
Special Guardian	
Final account	1885–1904
Guardianship Bonds	1880–1903
Records of Infants & Guardians	1876–1901
Probate Packets	1787–1921
Minutes of Wills	1839–1917
Minutes of Administration	1876–1903
Final settlements	1830–1860
Probate Court Records, Wills and Administrations, Ulster County, New York	1662–1783, 1787–1822[7]
Miscellaneous Papers, Accounts and Agreements, County Clerk	1718–1814

Published Records and Indexes

Anjou, Gustave. *Ulster County, New York, Probate Records in the Office of the Surrogate and in the County Clerk's Office at Kingston, New York: A Careful Abstract and Translation of the Dutch and English Wills, Letters of Administration after Intestates, and Inventories from 1665, with Genealogical and Historical Notes, and List of Dutch and Frisian Baptismal Names with Their English Equivalents.* 2 vols. New York: G. Anjou, 1906.[8]
❶FHL ◗LOC ◗NYPL ◗NYSL

Daughters of the American Revolution Magazine. Washington, D.C., 1913–).
Wills	1792–1793

Prehn, Florence. "Ulster Co., N.Y. Abstracts, Will Books, 1797–1836 (C, D, E, F, G, and H)" Typescript, [1898?]. ◗LOC ◗NYPL

Ulster County Genealogical Society. *Ulster Genie.* Stone Ridge, N.Y., 1976–)
◗FHL ◗NEHGS

Will Index	1791–1870
	23: 36; **24**: 10–11, 20–21, 33

---

[7] This FHLC entry was not broken down any further. The FHLC notes "Names only, arranged chronologically, 1662–1783 Wills, 1787–1822."

[8] See footnote 3 on page 9 for important information about Gustave Anjou's reputation as a genealogical forger.

Van Buren, Elizabeth R., and De Witt Van Buren, comp., *Abstracts of Wills of Ulster County Recorded at Kingston, New York, 1772–1813*. 3 vols. Typescript, 1941. ●FHL ⅡNYPL

Zimm, Louise Hasbrouck, trans. *Abstracts of Ulster County, New York, Will Books, E and F, 1814–1926 [1826]*. Typescript. Woodstock, N.Y., 1949–1950). ●FHL ⅡNYPL

Records on the Internet

New England Historic Genealogical Society
www.AmericanAncestors.org
> Abstracts of Wills, Administrations and Guardianships in NY State, 1787–1835 [database].

Sampubco
www.Sampubco.com
> Ulster County wills from 1817 to 1903 are indexed.

US Genweb Archives Project
www.usgwarchives.org
> Includes Sampubco's Testator Indexes and abstracts of some wills.

Warren County

Warren County Surrogate's Court

Warren County Municipal Center
1340 State Route 9
Lake George, NY 12845–9803

Phone	(518) 761–6512
Fax	(518) 761–6511
email	None
Hours	M–F 9:00 am to 5:00 pm
Website	www.nycourts.gov/courts/4jd/warren/surrogates.shtml

Date Formed	12 March 1813
County Seat	Lake George
Parent County	Washington

Records on Microfilm at the Family History Library

Records		Indexes
Wills	1813–1920	N/A
Administrations	1830–1917	
Letters of Administration and Testamentary	1830–1894	
Letters of Administration	1894–1917	
Letters of Testamentary	1894–1918	
Letters of adm. With Will Annexed	1894–1918	
Guardianship Letters	1815–1888	
Guardianship Appointments	1885–1916	
Special Guardianship Appointments	1902–1919	
Book of Judicial Settlements and Real Estate Sales	1885–1953	
Estate Papers	1813–1955	

Published Records and Indexes

Barber, Gertrude A., comp. Abstracts of Wills of Warren County, New York: Book A, 1813–1850. Typescript. New York [?], 1937). ●FHL ⫪LOC ⫪NYPL

Central New York Genealogical Society. *Tree Talks*. Syracuse, N.Y., 1961–.
⫪FHL ⫪NEHGS ⫪NYPL ⫪NYSL

Wills	1817–1837, 1839–1853	
	8: 170, 230; **9**: 57; **10**: 124, 187; **13**: 55–56, 178–9;	
	17: 47–48, 119–20; **18**: 59–60, 187–8; **19**: 121–2;	
	27: 185–6; **28**: 183–4; **29**: 185–6; **31**: 185–6; **33**: 183–4;	
	34: 183–4; **35**: 183–4; **36**: 183–4; **37**: 183–4; **38**: 183–4;	
	39: 181–2; **40**: 181–2; **41**: 181–2; **42**: 181–2; **43**: 181–2;	
	44: 181–2; **45**: 181–2	
Guardianships	1838–1868	
	5: 148, 199; **23**: 191–2; **45**: 182; **46**: 179–80; **47**: 181–2;	
	48: 181	

Samuelsen, W. David. *Warren County, New York Will Testators Index, 1813–1920*. Salt Lake City: Sampubco, 1996. ●FHL

Records on the Internet

New England Historic Genealogical Society
www.AmericanAncestors.org
Abstracts of Wills, Administrations and Guardianships in NY State, 1787–1835 [database].

NYGenWeb, Warren County
www.usgenweb.org
Abstracts of select Warren County wills.

Sampubco
www.Sampubco.com
Warren County wills from 1804 to 1904 are indexed.

US Genweb Archives Project
www.usgwarchives.org
Includes abstracts of some wills.

Washington County

Washington County Surrogate's Court

383 Broadway, Building C
Fort Edward, NY 12828

Phone	(518) 746–2545
Fax	(518) 746–2547
email	None
Hours	M–F 8:30 am to 4:30 pm
Website	www.nycourts.gov/courts/4jd/washington/index.shtml

Date Formed	12 March 1772
County Seat	Fort Edward
Parent County	Albany (created as Charlotte County; name changed 2 April 1784)

Washington County Archives

383 Broadway, Building A
Fort Edward, NY 12828

Phone	(518) 746–2136
Fax	None
Email	None
Hours	M–F 8:30 am to 4:30 pm
Website	None

Special Notes

Records of the Surrogate's Court prior to 1915 have been transferred to the Washington County Archives.

Records on Microfilm at the Family History Library

Records		Indexes	
Wills	1788–1916	1788–1896	
Administrations	1787–1916	1787–1892	
Letters testamentary	1788–1894		

Records (cont.)		Indexes (cont.)
Decrees	1872–1902	
Orders Admitting [Wills] to Probate	1872–1885	
Letters of Guardianship	1818–1828	
Decrees of Guardianship	1896–1928	
General Minutes	1830–1900	1830–1836
Probate Packets	N/A	

Published Records and Indexes

Barber, Gertrude A., comp. *Abstracts of Wills at Washington County, New York: Copied from the Original Records at the Surrogate's Office, Salem, New York.* 3 vols. in 1. Typescript. New York [?], 1937). ⬤FHL ◪FHL ◪LOC ◪NEHGS ◪NYPL ◪NYSL

———. *Index of Wills of Washington County, New York, 1825–1890.* 3 vols. in 2. Typescript: New York [?], 1937–1959). ⬤FHL ◪LOC ◪NYPL ◪NYSL

Central New York Genealogical Society. *Tree Talks.* Syracuse, N.Y., 1961–. ◪FHL ◪NEHGS ◪NYPL ◪NYSL

Wills	1802–1804
	7: 53, 108, 161, 216; **20**: 128, 191; **21**: 64, 191
Letters of Admin	1797–1825
	37: 185–6
Administrations	1790–1807, 1810–1825
	12: 115–6, 231–2; **13**: 112; **17**: 50–52; **20**: 127–8; **32**: 186; **33**: 185–6; **34**: 185–6; **35**: 185–6; **36**: 185–6; **38**: 185; **44**: 183–4; **45**: 183–4; **46**: 181–2; **47**: 183–4; **48**: 183–4; **49**: 61–62, 185–6

Samuelsen, W. David. *Washington County, New York Will Testators Index, 1788–1916.* Salt Lake City: Sampubco, 1996. ⬤FHL

Shepard, Charles. "Abstracts of Wills Proved in the Court of Common Pleas of Rensselaer County, New York, from 1794 to 1822, Together With One Will from Washington County, New York." Typescript. Troy, N.Y., 1921). ⬤FHL ◪LOC ◪NEHGS ◪NYSL

Records on the Internet

New England Historic Genealogical Society
www.AmericanAncestors.org
Abstracts of Wills, Administrations and Guardianships in NY State, 1787–1835 [database].

NYGenWeb, Washington County
www.usgenweb.org
Abstracts of select Washington County wills.

Sampubco

www.Sampubco.com

Washington County wills from 1804 to 1904 are indexed.

US Genweb Archives Project

www.usgwarchives.org

Includes abstracts of some wills.

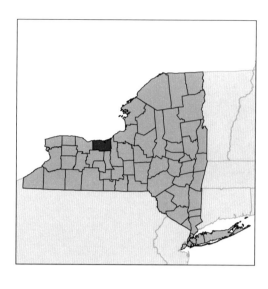

Wayne County

Wayne County Surrogate's Court

Hall of Justice
54 Broad Street, Ste. 106
Lyons, NY 14489

Date Formed	11 April 1823
County Seat	Lyons
Parent County	Ontario/Seneca

Phone   (315) 946–5430
Fax   (315) 946–5433
email   None
Hours   M–F 9:00 am to 5:00 pm
Website   www.nycourts.gov/courts/7jd/courts/surrogates

Wayne County Historian

Peter Evans, Director
Office of Tourism/History
9 Pearl Street, Suite 3
Lyons, NY 14489

Phone   (315) 946–5470
Fax   None
Email   None
Hours   M–F 9:00 am to 12:00 noon, 1:00 pm to 5:00 pm
Website   www.co.wayne.ny.us/departments/historian/historian.htm

Special Notes

Earlier probate records have been microfilmed and are available for research at the surrogate court office. Original paper records are archived at the Wayne County Historian's
office and are available for research. Written requests to the County Historian's office
are subject to a research fee of $20/hour for searches, with a $10 minimum charge, plus
copy expenses. No search charge for Wayne County residents. Include authorization
for maximum number of hours to be allowed in search (usual is 1–2 hours). Wills and
estate records from 1823 to the current year are in the custody of the county historian.

Records on Microfilm at the Family History Library

Records		Indexes	
Wills	1823–1901	Surrogates	1823–1964
Administrations	1823–1903		
Letters Testamentary			
& of Administration	1830–1903		
Letters Testamentary	1859–1902		
Bonds	1890–1897		
Guardianships Letters	1823–1860		
Guardianships	1871–1890		
Minutes, Orders, &			
Decrees	1854–1879		
Judicial settlements	1883–1903		
Final settlements	1855–1883		
Probate Packets	N/A		

Published Records and Indexes

Central New York Genealogical Society. *Tree Talks.* Syracuse, N.Y., 1961–.
▮FHL **▮**NEHGS **▮**NYPL **▮**NYSL

Wills   1823–1831
8: 232; **15**: 81–82, 163–4; **16**: 55–56; **17**: 53–54; **18**: 16–17;
19: 123–4; **23**: 64; **25**: 123–4; **34**: 125–6, 187; **47**: 185–6;
48: 125–6, 185–6; **49**: 125–6, 187–8

Wiles, Harriett M. *Abstracts of Wills of Wayne County, New York, Libers A-H, 1823–1859: Copied from Surrogate's Office, Lyons, New York.* 4 vols. in 1. Typescript.
●FHL **▮**NYPL **▮**NYSL

―――. *Letters of Administration, 1823–1850: Intestate Records of Wayne County, New York, in Surrogate's Office.* 2 vols. in 1. Typescript, 1939–1940. **▮**NYPL

Records on the Internet

New England Historic Genealogical Society
www.AmericanAncestors.org
Abstracts of Wills, Administrations and Guardianships in NY State, 1787–1835 [database].

Sampubco
www.Sampubco.com
Wayne County wills from 1823 to 1901 are indexed.

US Genweb Archives Project
www.usgwarchives.org
Includes the Sampubco indexes and abstracts of some wills.

Westchester County

Westchester County Surrogate's Court

111 Dr. Martin Luther King Jr. Blvd,
19th floor
White Plains, NY 10601

Phone	(914) 824–5656
Fax	(914) 995–3728
email	None
Hours	M–F 9:00 am to 5:00 pm
Website	www.nycourts.gov/courts/9jd/Westchester/surrogates.shtml

Date Formed	1 November 1683
County Seat	White Plains
Parent County	Original

Westchester County Archives

2199 Saw Mill River Road
Elmsford, NY 10523

Phone	(914) 231–1500
Fax	None
email	None
Hours	T–W only, 9 am to 4 pm
Website	www.westchestergov.com/wcarchives

Special Notes

Researchers must request file petitions before 3:30 pm. Most files are stored offsite and may take several days for personnel to access them. Make arrangements in advance to review records at the office. Check for summer hours. All original records prior to 1914 are at the county archives.

Records on Microfilm at the Family History Library

Records		Indexes	
Wills	1787–1915	Surrogates	1813[9]–1983
Letters Testamentary	1830–1900		
Letters of Administration	1777–1905		
Letters of Guardianship	1802–1900		
Estate Tax Files	1775–1900		
Probate Packets	See Estate Tax Files		

Published Records and Indexes

Fox, Dixon Ryan, ed. *The Minutes of the Court of Sessions (1657–1696), Westchester County, New York.* White Plains, N.Y.: Westchester County Historical Society, 1924. ∎FHL ∎NEHGS

"Lists of Original Wills of Westchester County in the Surrogate's Office, 1777–1812." Typescript. ●FHL

New York Genealogical and Biographical Society. *New York Genealogical and Biographical Record.* New York, 1870–. ∎FHL ∎NEHGS ∎NYPL ∎NYSL

Wills	1787–1811
	55: 143–54, 262–69, 330–38; **56**: 118–26; **57**: 5–10, 102–07; 248–53, 320–25; **58**: 40–44, 143–49, 202–08; 381–88; **60**: 149–55
Administrations	1787–1812
	59: 26–32, 130–36
Unrecorded Wills	1793–1798
	67: 75–76

Pelletreau, William S. *Early Wills of Westchester County, New York, 1664–1784: A Careful Abstract of All Wills (Nearly 800) Recorded in New York Surrogate's Office and at White Plains, New York, from 1664–1784; Also the Genealogy of the "Havilands" of Westchester County and Descendants of Hon. James Graham (Watkinson and Ackerly Families) with Genealogical and Historical Notes.* New York: Harper, 1898. ●FHL ∎NEHGS ∎NYPL ∎NYSL

Larchmont Chapter. "Abstracts of Wills for the township of Scarsdale, Westchester County, New York, 1788 to 1855." *New York DAR Genealogical Records Committee Report,* series 3, volume 108 (1955). ●FHL ∎DAR

———. "Unpublished Wills of Westchester County." *New York DAR Genealogical Records Committee Report,* series 3, volume 103 (1953). ●FHL ∎DAR

---

[9] FHLC says 1813, but earlier records are indexed.

Records on the Internet

New England Historic Genealogical Society

www.AmericanAncestors.org

Abstracts of Wills, Administrations and Guardianships in NY State, 1787–1835 [database].

Sampubco

www.Sampubco.com

Westchester County wills from 1787 to 1843 are indexed (in progress).

US Genweb Archives Project

www.usgwarchives.org

Includes abstracts of some wills.

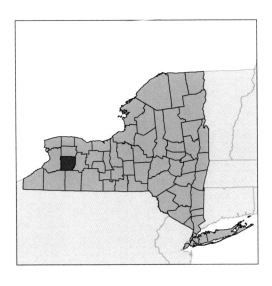

Wyoming County

Wyoming County Surrogate's Court

147 North Main Street
Warsaw, NY 14569

Phone	(585) 786–3148
Fax	(585) 786–3800
email	None
Hours	M–F 9:00 am to 5:00 pm
Website	www.nycourts.gov/courts/8jd/wyoming/index.shtml

Date Formed	19 May 1841
County Seat	Warsaw
Parent County	Genesee

Special Notes

Make arrangements in advance to review records at their office. Some records are archived in the basement. Will petitions and administration petitions are in books and on film.

Records on Microfilm at the Family History Library

Records

Record of Wills	1841–1918
Petitions and Proofs of Wills	1841–1900
Letters Testamentary	1841–1901
Letters of Administration	1841–1908
Administration Orders	1871–1904
Testamentary Orders	1869–1905
Petitions and Bonds of Administration	1841–1900
Administration with Will annexed, vol. 1	1882–1959
Probate of Heirship, Guardians Petitions & Bonds	1841–1900

Indexes

Surrogates	1886–1906

Records (cont.)

General Guardians	1883–1969
Guardian Bonds	1890–1912
Guardian Letters & Orders	1841–1877
Special Guardians, Letters, & Orders	1857–1903
General Guardians orders	1882–1884
Letters of Guardianship	1869–1884
Dowers of Guardianship	1841–1871
Dowers Proceedings	1841–1900
Settlements	1841–1900
Decrees of Settlements	1884–1900
Real Estate Proceedings	1842–1899
Inventories	1841–1900
Estate and Transfer Tax Proceedings	1887–1900
Probate Orders, Letters, Bonds	1841–1969
Probate Packets	See Petitions
Miscellaneous records (County Clerk)	1841–1929
Miscellaneous record (Surrogate)	1841–1902

Published Records and Indexes

Central New York Genealogical Society. *Tree Talks.* Syracuse, N.Y., 1961–.
∎FHL ∎NEHGS ∎NYPL ∎NYSL

Wills	1841–1842
	23: 125–6; **24**: 127–8; **47**: 187–8; **48**: 187–8
Administrations	1841–1856
	26: 189–90; **27**: 191–2; **31**: 191; **34**: 189–90; **41**: 187–8;
	42: 187–8; **43**: 187–8; **44**: 187–8; **45**: 187–8; **46**: 185–6
Dower	1841–1861
	13: 241; **14**: 117–8; **15**: 83; **18**: 189–90; **24**: 128; **25**: 125

Samuelsen, W. David. *Wyoming County, New York Probate Records, 1841–1900.* North Salt Lake, Utah: AISI, 1988. ∎NYPL

Records on the Internet

NYGenWeb, Wyoming County
www.usgenweb.org

Contains a direct link to the Sampubco Testator Indexes.

Sampubco

www.Sampubco.com

Wyoming County wills from 1804 to 1904 are indexed.

US Genweb Archives Project

www.usgwarchives.org

Includes abstracts of some wills.

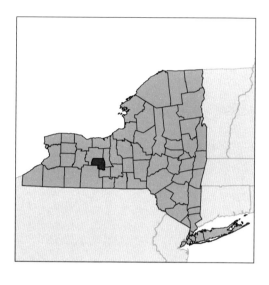

Yates County

Yates County Surrogate's Court

415 Liberty Street
Penn Yan, NY 14527

Phone   (315) 536–5130
Fax   (315) 536–5190
email   None
Hours   M–F 9:00 am to 5:00 pm
         M–F 8:30 am to 4:30 pm (summer)
Website www.nycourts.gov/courts/7jd/courts/surrogates

Date Formed	5 February 1823
County Seat	Penn Yan
Parent County	Ontario

Records on Microfilm at the Family History Library

Records		Indexes	
Wills	1823–1903	Surrogates	1823–1951
Letters of Testamentary and of Administration	1823–1904		
Administrative Orders	1863–1905		
Administrative bonds	1890–1906		
Guardianships	1823–1894		
Dower Record	1827–1879		
Minutes, Order, & Decrees	1830–1901		
Real Estate	1824–1906		
Renunciation	1852–1939		
Probate Packets	N/A		

Published Records and Indexes

Bootes, Mrs. Fenton E. for Daughters of the American Colonists, GA–HA–DA Chapter (Seneca Falls, New York). "Deans of Morris Co., Wantage, New Jersey (Index Will Book A, B, C—Penn Yan, Yates County N.Y." Typescript. ●FHL

Central New York Genealogical Society. *Tree Talks.* Syracuse, N.Y., 1961–).
⊠FHL **⊠**NEHGS **⊠**NYPL **⊠**NYSL

Wills	1823–1835
	8: 174, 234; **9**: 60; **13**: 242–3; **14**: 119–20; **24**: 191–2;
	25: 127–8; **33**: 191–2; **34**: 191–2; **35**: 191–2; **36**: 191–2;
	37: 191; **40**: 189–90; **41**: 189
Guardianships	1823–1844
	41: 190; **42**: 189; **43**: 189–90; **44**: 189–90; **45**: 189–90;
	46: 187–8; **47**: 189–90; **48**: 189–90; **49**: 189–90

Records on the Internet

New England Historic Genealogical Society
www.AmericanAncestors.org

Abstracts of Wills, Administrations and Guardianships in NY State, 1787–1835 [database].

NYGenWeb, Yates County
www.usgenweb.org

Contains an every name index to Yates County Will Books and an alphabetical index to principals and heirs.

Sampubco
www.Sampubco.com

Yates County wills from 1823 to 1903 are indexed.

US Genweb Archives Project
www.usgwarchives.org

Includes abstracts of some wills.

Appendixes

Appendix A: New York Counties

County/ Date Formed	County Seat	Parent County/ Counties	Daughter County/ Counties	Part Annexed from/Ceded to
Albany Nov. 1, 1683	Albany	Original county	Cumberland, *defunct* (1766) Greene (1800) Gloucester, *defunct* (1770) Tryon, *now Montgomery* (1772) Charlotte, *now Washington* (1772) Rensselaer (1791) Saratoga (1791) Schenectady (1809)	*Part ceded to* Schoharie (1795)
Allegany Apr. 7, 1806	Belmont	Genesee		*Part annexed from* Steuben (1808) *Part ceded to* Genesee (1811) Wyoming (1846) Livingston (1846)
Bronx Apr. 19, 1912	Bronx Borough, NYC	New York		
Broome Mar. 28, 1806	Binghamton	Tioga (1806)		*Part ceded to* Tioga (1822)
Cattaraugus Mar. 11, 1808	Ellicottville (1808–60) Little Valley (1860–pres.)	Genesee		
Cayuga Mar. 8, 1799	Auburn	Onondaga	Seneca (1804) Tompkins (1817)	

County/ Date Formed	County Seat	Parent County/ Counties	Daughter County/ Counties	Part Annexed from/Ceded to
Charlotte *see* Washington				
Chautauqua (Chautauque) Mar. 11, 1808	Mayville	Genesee		
Chemung Mar. 29, 1836	Elmira	Tioga	Schuyler (1854)	
Chenango Mar. 15, 1798	Norwich	Herkimer, Tioga	Madison (1804)	*Part ceded to* Oneida (1804)
Clinton Mar. 7, 1788	Plattsburgh	Washington, St. Lawrence (annexed 1801)	Essex (1799) St. Lawrence (1802) Franklin (1808)	
Columbia Apr. 4, 1786	Hudson	Albany		
Cortland Apr. 8, 1808	Cortland	Onondaga		
Cumberland July 3, 1766 *defunct*		Albany		*Ceded to* Vermont (1777)
Delaware Mar. 10, 1797	Delhi	Ulster Otsego		
Dutchess Nov. 1, 1683	Poughkeepsie	Original county	Putnam (1812)	*Part ceded to* Albany (1717)
Erie Apr. 2, 1821	Buffalo	Niagara		
Essex Mar. 1, 1799	Elizabeth-town	Clinton	Franklin (1808)	
Franklin Mar. 11, 1808	Malone	Clinton Essex		*Part ceded to* Essex (1822)
Fulton Apr. 18, 1838	Johnstown	Montgomery		

County/ Date Formed	County Seat	Parent County/ Counties	Daughter County/ Counties	Part Annexed from/Ceded to
Genesee Mar. 30, 1802	Batavia	Ontario	Allegany (1806) Cattaraugus (1808) Chautauqua (1808) Niagara (1808) Livingston (1821) Monroe (1821) Orleans (1824) Wyoming (1841)	*Part ceded to* Livingston (1823) Orleans (1825)
Gloucester Mar. 16, 1770 *defunct*		Albany		*Ceded to* Vermont (1777)
Greene Mar. 25, 1800	Catskill	Albany, Ulster		*Part ceded to* Ulster (1812)
Hamilton Feb. 12, 1816	Sageville Lake Pleasant	Montgomery		
Herkimer Feb. 16, 1791	Herkimer	Montgomery	Onandaga (1794) Oneida (1798) Chenango (1798) St. Lawrence (1802)	*Part annexed from* Montgomery (1817) Otsego (1816) Plainfield (1816) Richfield (1816) *Part ceded to* Montgomery (1797)
Jefferson Mar. 28, 1805	Watertown	Oneida		*Part annexed from* Lewis (1813) *Part ceded to* Lewis (1809)
Kings Nov. 1, 1683	Brooklyn Borough, NYC	Original county		
Lewis Mar. 28, 1805	Lowville	Oneida		
Livingston Feb. 23, 1821	Geneseo	Genesee Ontario		*Part annexed from* Allegany (1846, 1856)

County/ Date Formed	County Seat	Parent County/ Counties	Daughter County/ Counties	Part Annexed from/Ceded to
Madison Mar. 21, 1806	Wampsville	Madison		*Part annexed from* Oneida (1836)
Monroe Feb. 23, 1821	Rochester	Genesee Ontario		
Montgomery (founded as Tryon Mar. 12, 1772; name changed Apr. 2, 1784)	Fonda	Albany	Ontario (1789) Herkimer (1791) Otsego (1791) Tioga (1791) St. Lawrence (1802) Hamilton (1816) Fulton (1838)	
Nassau Jan. 1, 1899	Mineola	Queens		
New York Nov. 1, 1683	Manhattan Borough, NYC	Original county	Westchester (1874)	
Niagara Mar. 11, 1808	Lockport	Genesee	Erie (1821)	
Oneida Mar. 15, 1798	Utica	Herkimer	Lewis (1805) Jefferson (1805) Oswego (1816)	*Part annexed from* Chenango (1804) *Part ceded to* Clinton (1801) Madison (1836)
Onondaga Mar. 5, 1794	Syracuse	Herkimer	Cayuga (1799) Cortland (1808) Oswego (1816)	
Ontario Jan. 27, 1789	Canandaigua	Montgomery	Steuben (1796) Genesee (1802) Livingston (1821) Monroe (1821) Wayne (1823) Yates (1823)	*Part annexed from* Montgomery (1791) Steuben (1814)
Orange Nov. 1, 1683	Goshen	Original county	Rockland (1798)	*Part annexed from* Ulster (1798)

County/ Date Formed	County Seat	Parent County/ Counties	Daughter County/ Counties	Part Annexed from/Ceded to
Orleans Nov. 11, 1824	Albion	Genesee		*Part annexed from* Genesee (1825)
Oswego Mar. 1, 1816	Oswego Pulaski	Oneida Onondaga		
Otsego Feb. 16, 1791	Cooperstown	Montgomery	Scoharie (1795) Delaware (1797)	
Putnam June 12, 1812	Carmel	Dutchess		
Queens Nov. 1, 1683	Queens Borough, NYC	Original county		
Rensselaer Feb. 7, 1791	Troy	Albany		
Richmond Nov. 1, 1683	Staten Island Borough, NYC	Original county		
Rockland Feb. 23, 1798	New City	Orange		
St. Lawrence Mar. 3, 1802	Ogdensburgh (1802–28) Canton (1828–pres.)	Clinton Montgomery Herkimer		
Saratoga Feb. 7, 1791	Ballston Spa	Albany		
Schenectady Mar. 7, 1809	Schenectady	Albany		
Schoharie Apr. 6, 1795	Schoharie	Albany Otsego		*Part annexed from* Greene (1836)
Schuyler Apr. 17, 1854	Watkins Glen	Chemung Steuben Tompkins		

County/ Date Formed	County Seat	Parent County/ Counties	Daughter County/ Counties	Part Annexed from/Ceded to
Seneca Mar. 29, 1804	Ovid Waterloo	Cayuga	Tompkins (1817) Wayne (1823)	*Part annexed from* Tompkins (1819)
Steuben Mar. 18, 1796	Bath	Ontario	Yates (1823) Schuyler (1854)	*Part annexed from* Allegany (1808) Livingston (1821)
Suffolk Nov. 1, 1683	Riverhead	Original county		
Sullivan Mar. 27, 1809	Monticello	Ulster	Ulster (1809)	
Tioga Feb. 16, 1791	Owego	Montgomery	Chenango (1798) Broome (1806) Tompkins (1822) Chemung (1836)	
Tompkins Apr. 17, 1817	Ithaca	Cayuga Seneca	Schuyler (1854)	
Tryon *see* Montgomery				
Ulster Nov. 1, 1683	Kingston	Original county	Delaware (1798) Greene (1808) Sullivan (1809)	
Warren Mar. 12, 1813	Lake George	Washington		
Washington Mar. 12, 1772 (name change Apr. 2, 1784) (1790)	Hudson Falls (until 1994) Ft. Edward (1994–pres.)	Albany	Clinton (1788) Warren (1813)	*Part annexed from* Albany (1791) *Part ceded to* State of Vt.
Wayne Apr. 11, 1823	Lyons	Ontario Seneca		
Westchester Nov. 1, 1683	White Plains	Original county		*Part ceded to* New York County (1874, 1895)

County/ Date Formed	County Seat	Parent County/ Counties	Daughter County/ Counties	Part Annexed from/Ceded to
Wyoming May 14, 1841	Warsaw	Genesee		*Part annexed from* Allegany (1846)
Yates Feb. 5, 1823	Penn Yan	Ontario		*Part annexed from* Steuben (1824)

Appendix B: Defunct New York Counties

The original counties of New York were created in 1683. These included the modern counties of Albany, Dutchess, Orange, Ulster, Kings, New York, Queens, Richmond, Suffolk, and Westchester — plus two now extinct counties, Cornwall and Dukes. Two other counties, Tryon and Charlotte, changed their names.

Cumberland County was created from Albany County in 1766. Gloucester County was created from Albany County in 1770. These two counties, as well as parts of Albany and Charlotte (now Washington) Counties, were part of disputed territory between New York and New Hampshire. Both colonies laid claim to the territory around the Connecticut River. Residents of the area fought both colonies, and in 1777 these counties were ceded to Vermont.

Cornwall County was established in 1665 from land granted to the Duke of York. The grant ran from the St. Lawrence River to the Atlantic Ocean, between the Kennebec and St. Croix Rivers. In 1687 the county was transferred to the Dominion of New England.

Settled in 1641 as part of the Massachusetts Bay Company's territory, the area of Martha's Vineyard, Nantucket, and the surrounding islands was transferred to New York in 1665. In 1683 it became Dukes County. In 1691 the land was transferred to Massachusetts.

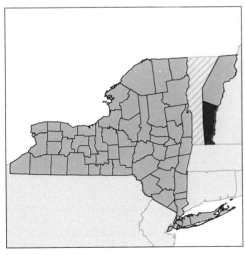

Cumberland County

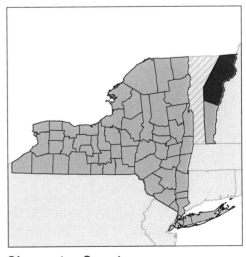

Gloucester County

Estates in Cornwall and Dukes counties should have been handled in local courts of session (under £100) or transmitted to the Secretary of the Province in New York City (over £100). The remoteness of the counties may have caused estates to be handled locally.

After the creation of Prerogative Court of New York in 1691, almost all estates, including those of now-defunct counties, should have been probated in New York City.

Tryon County, New York, was created in 1772 from Albany County. In 1784 the name was changed to Montgomery County. Charlotte County was also formed in 1772 from Albany County. In 1784 the name was changed to Washington County.

There are also cases where persons living in what is now New York State may have considered themselves under the jurisdiction of another government. This is true of English settlers on Long Island and the Massachusetts squatters in Nobletown and Spencertown in what is now Columbia County, New York. Records pertaining to them might be found in New Haven County, Connecticut, or in the counties of Hampshire and Berkshire in Massachusetts. Likewise, there may be cases where persons living in neighboring colonies, such as those claimed by the Duke of York (Delaware, parts of New Jersey, and the aforementioned counties of Cornwall and Dukes), had their estates probated in New York.

As a general genealogical research principle, one should be aware of county boundary changes. While such changes should not affect the probate of estates in New York between 1691 and 1787 (the establishment of surrogate's courts in each county), there be could confusion about the residence of the decedent or places mentioned in a will

For instance, William Betts of the "Yonckers Plantation, in the Jurisdiction now of New Orange so called" made his will on "The Twelfth day of the Twelfth month 1673."[1] At this time New York had been re-occupied by the Dutch and renamed "New Orange." The will of William Betts was probated in New York City on January 2, 1675 — after the return to English rule. It is found in the records of the Surrogate's Court of New York County even though that county did not yet exist and neither did the Prerogative Court of New York.

An excellent source for county boundary changes, created by the Newberry Library of Chicago, can be found at the website *http://historicalcounty.newberry.org/website/New_York/viewer.htm*. Much of the information in the following table was drawn from this website.

---

[1] "Abstracts of Wills on File in the Surrogate's Office, City of New York, Vol. I, 1677-1708," in *Collections of the New York Historical Society for the Year 1892*, Vol. 25, pp. 33-34.

County Name	Location	Date Created	Date Ended	
Cornwall	Duke of York's grant in present Maine and Quebec, including the Pemaquid settlement governed since 1674 by Massachusetts	1683	1687	Ceded to the Dominion of New England
Dukes	Created to cover the 1674 grant to the Duke of York of islands in Massachusetts, including Martha's Vineyard, Nantucket, and Elizabeth Islands	1683	1691	Ceded to Province of Massachusetts Bay
Cumberland	Vermont	1766	1777	Ceded to Vermont
Gloucester	Vermont	1770	1777	Ceded to Vermont
Charlotte	New York	1772	1784	Name changed to Washington
Tryon	New York	1772	1784	Name changed to Montgomery

Appendix C:
Organizations Helpful in Research

Many organizations have holdings and publications that will assist you in researching New York Probate records. The following organizations will be of significant assistance:

Family History Library
35 North West Temple
Salt Lake City, UT 84150
www.familysearch.org

New England Historic Genealogical Society
101 Newbury Street
Boston, Massachusetts 02116
(617) 536-5740
onlinegenealogist@nehgs.org
www.AmericanAncestors.org

New York Genealogical and Biographical Society
36 West 44th Street, 7th Floor
New York, New York 10036-8105
(212) 755-8532
membership@nygbs.org
www.newyorkfamilyhistory.org

New York Public Library
Milstein Division of U.S. History, Local History, & Genealogy
Stephen A. Schwarzman Building, Room 121
Fifth Avenue & 42 Street
New York, New York 10018
(212) 930-0828
histref@nypl.org
www.nypl.org

New York State Archives
Cultural Education Center
222 Madison Avenue
Albany, New York 12230
(518)474-8955
archref@mail.nysed.gov
www.archives.nysed.gov

New York State Library
Cultural Education Center
222 Madison Avenue
Albany, New York 12230
(518) 474-5355
nyslweb@mail.nysed.gov
www.nysl.nysed.gov

Appendix D:
Abstracted Early New York State Probate Material

Abstracts of Wills, 17 vols., Colls. NYHS: will books 1665-1787 (incl. administrations before 1743; administrations 1743-1783 listed separately); unrecorded wills in vol. 11; index to testators and intestates in Kelly, *Index to Principals*. Wills and administrations for New York Co. only 1787-1800 in vols. 14-15 (see p. 19–22).

NYSA series included in *Abstracts of Wills*

- J0043-92 will books 1665-1787; incl. administration before 1743; index to testators in Sawyer, *Index to Wills, 1662-1850*.

- J0038-92 original wills 1665-1787 (most in vol. 11 of *Abstracts of Wills*); index to testators in Scott, NGSQ 51: 90-99, 174-78, 185; 54: 98-124; 55: 119-45.

- J1032-04 administrations 1743-1783; index by Barber, *Index to Letters of Administration, 1743-1875*.

FHL film or fiche

- *Abstracts of Wills*   yes, and FHLC digital
- Sawyer, *Index to Wills, 1662-1850*   yes
- Barber, *Index to Letters, 1743-1875*   yes
- J0043-92   yes
- J0038-92   yes, but not ca. 1739-1787
- J1032-04   yes

Fernow, Calendar of Wills, 1626–1836: wills from six collections now at NYSA plus Albany Co. wills (see p. 3, 10); on *AmericanAncestors.org* for non-members.

NYSA series included in *Calendar of Wills*

- J0038-82 wills 1671-1815, mostly for testators north of NYC; some duplication of wills found in J0043-92 and J0038-92, listed above; cited with a letter and number code in *Calendar of Wills*.

- J0043-85 wills and probates 1787-1822; cited as vols. I and II in *Calendar of Wills*.

- J0039-85 wills and letters of administration 1783-1801; cited as vol. III in *Calendar of Wills*.

- J0041-85 wills proved at Albany (Supreme Court of Judicature), 1799-1829; cited as vol. IV in *Calendar of Wills.*
- J0020-82 wills proved at Utica (Supreme Court of Judicature), 1818-1829; cited as vol. V in *Calendar of Wills.*

FHL film or fiche

- *Calendar of Wills*   yes
- J0038-82   yes
- J0043-85   yes
- J0039-85   yes
- J0041-85   yes
- J0020-82   yes

Scott, *Administration Papers* [ca. 1700-1823].

NYSA series included in *Administration Papers*

- J0033-82 administration papers ca. 1700-1823.

FHL film or fiche

- *Administration Papers*   no
- J0033-82   no

Scott, *Administration Bonds and Letters of Administration* 1753-1799, and Scott, *Further Administration Bonds* 1791-1798.

NYSA series included in *Administration Bonds and Letters of Administration*

- J1033-04 administration bonds, 1753-1798.
- J0032-83, -85 letters of administration 1778-1823 (only to 1799 in *Administration Bonds and Letters of Administration*, whose contents are only partly from the New York State Archives).

FHL film or fiche

Administration Bonds and Letters of Administration	no
J1033-04	yes
J0032-83	yes
J0032-85	yes

Scott and Owre, *Inventories, 1666-1825:* indexed in part up to 1775 in Scott, NGSQ 53: 133-38; 54: 246-59.

NYSA series included in Scott and Owre, *Inventories, 1666-1825*

- J0301-82 inventories and accounts, 1666-1822.
- J1301-04 estate inventories, 1730-1753.

FHL film or fiche

- *Inventories, 1666-1825*   no
- J0301-82   yes
- J1301-04   yes

Scott, *Guardianships from the Chancery Court, 1691-1815*.

NYSA series included in Scott, *Guardianships, 1691-1815*

- none

FHL film or fiche

- *Guardianships, 1691–1815* yes

Sawyer, "Abstract of Wills Probated in the Common Pleas Court (also known as Mayor's Court), 1817-1892, Supreme Court of Judicature, 1821 [*sic*, actually 1787]-1829 . . .," typescript, 1948

NYSA series included in Sawyer, "Abstract of Wills Probated"

- J2041-04 wills proved at NYC (Supreme Court of Judicature), 1787-1829

FHL film or fiche

- "Abstract of Wills Probated"   yes
- J2041-04   yes

Probate Material in the New York State Archives That Has Not Been Abstracted (mostly after 1787)

- J0039-04   letters testamentary, 1793-1801
- J0042-04   list of documents delivered, 1799
- J2301-04   estate inventories, 1779-1786
- J0208-82   orders and decrees, 1811-1823
- J0040-82   wills proved in Court of Chancery, 1830-1848
- J0040-85   wills proved in Court of Chancery, 1830-1848
- B0081-92   letters of administration and wills in Secretary of State's Office, 1823-1966

FHL film or fiche

- J0039-04   no [but Folts says yes]
- J0042-04   no [but Folts says yes]
- J2301-04   yes
- J0208-82   no
- J0040-82   yes
- J0040-85   yes
- B0081-92   no

Appendix E:
Working with Published Records

Published abstracts are valuable resources, and can narrow the search for the correct probate record in original documents. Perhaps the most comprehensive abstracting of all manner of New York probate records can be found in the Central New York Genealogical Society's periodical *Tree Talks*. In almost all cases, the abstracts were made by volunteers from the original records at the county surrogate's offices. According to one long-time member of the Central New York Genealogical Society:

> This has been done since the Central New York Genealogical Society started *Tree Talks*. It has been a struggle at times to get someone in certain counties to assist with the abstracting, but at the present there is a group who goes out and does it during the good weather months. If FHL microfilms were used the fact has been noted. Since the early 1960s, volunteers have been going to the county surrogate's office and personally abstracting the records.[1]

The abstracts in *Tree Talks* have a double pagination. One is a page number for the county in which the abstract is found. The second is a "serial" page number for the volume of *Tree Talks* in which the abstract appears. Some libraries have combined the county pages into county volumes, other libraries, such as FHL and NEHGS, have bound the issues of *Tree Talks* in its original serial volumes.

There are several name indexes to *Tree Talks*. From 2002 to 2005, Kinship Press of Rhinebeck, New York combined the county pages into "County Packets" and indexed each packet. Kinship published an *Every Name Index to the 49 Tree Talks County Packets (CNYGS) published 2002–2005*. The page numbers in these indexes are to the county pages, not the serial volume pages. In 2003 Kinship produced a name index on CD Rom in PDF Format covering the county packets from 1961 to 2001. This index also references only the county pages. This CD Rom is no longer listed in the Kinship Catalog.

The Central New York Genealogical Society has its own "*Tree Talks* "County Packets" Index Project" online at *www.rootsweb.ancestry.com/~nycnygs/index-master.htm*. This online index is a work in progress and not as complete as the indexes published by Kinship. It does, however, give both the county page and the serial volume page.

---

[1] Email from Gerald Parsons, FASG, Syracuse, New York, 1 March 2002.

The abstracts in *Tree Talks* cover not only wills and administrations, but guardianships and dower proceedings. This is an ongoing process, so the most recent issues of *Tree Talks* should be consulted for the newest abstracts.

Regardless of the wide availability of abstracts of probate records, one should always be careful of them and use them only as a guide to get to the original record. Two case studies of will abstracts from Schoharie County illustrate this principle. Schoharie County wills were abstracted by the prolific Gertrude A. Barber in 1938. These abstracts are available in typescript form and on microfilm at numerous repositories. In the first case, Barber abstracted the will of Wilhelmus Posson, giving the following information:[2]

Will of Wilhelmus Posson of Wirght [*sic*]

Dated Sept, 26, 1846. Probated June 8, 1847
Mentions: Wife   Anna
    Daus: Eliza, wife of Rensselaer Cross
               Caty, wife of David Becker
               Wealthy Ann Posson
    Sons: Daniel and George

Examination of the actual will revealed that Barber omitted a son, Peter Posson.[3]

Other errors can also occur. Names can be misread, relationships misinterpreted, and valuable clues deemed insignificant by the abstractor may be omitted. The will of George Handy, which closely preceded that of Wilhelmus Posson, was abstracted as follows:[4]

Will of George Handy of Schoharie
Dated Apr 25, 1845. Codicil Oct 1, 1845. Prob. May 10, 1847
Mentions: wife Elizabeth
       Sons: Nathaniel, Levi, and Levi's wife Sarah
       Grandson: George Jr., son of Nathaniel
       Trustees: Seth Eldridge, Julius Warner
Daus of Levi Handy: Priscilla, wife of Christian Shawl, Luancy, wife of Chancello Livingston, Sarah, Rebecca, and Susan Handy
Mentions [no relationships stated in abstract]:
Elizabeth, wife of Peter Ham
Jedediah Elsworth (single)
Jonathan Elsworth

Examination of the original will revealed the following differences and/or omissions:[5]

---

[2]   Gertrude A. Barber, comp. "Abstracts of Wills, Letters of Administration, Letters of Guardianship, of Schoharie County, New York, 1795–1863" (typescript; New York [?], 1938) 3:45.

[3]   Schoharie County, New York ,Wills, B: 248.

[4]   Barber, "Abstracts Schoharie County," 3:44 [see note 1].

[5]   Schoharie County, New York, Wills, B: 239.

George Handy was of the town of Sharon, Schoharie County. Since there is a town of Schoharie in Schoharie County, the lack of a named town in the abstract could potentially create confusion for the user. "Luancy" Livingston's first name *is* difficult to decipher in the actual will, but her husband was definitely "Chancellor" not "Chancello"

More significantly, a valuable clue was hidden in his bequest to wife Elizabeth. She was to receive, among other property, "all the household furniture that has been purchased since I married her." This implies that she may not have been his first wife. Since at least two of George's daughters were married (indicating that he was of an age to have grandchildren), this is a reasonable hypothesis.

"Jedediah" Elsworth was actually "Jedida Elsworth" and not only a female, but also the wife of Jonathan Elsworth and therefore not single. The abstract also left out several mentions of George Handy's daughter "Jedide" or "Jedidah Clumb."

The implication that Elizabeth was not George Handy's first wife combined with the unusual female name "Jedidah" raises the possibility that he was the George Handy who married Jedidah Hammond at New Bedford, Massachusetts, on 25 June 1791.[6] Thus, the omission in the abstract of the daughter Jedidah Clumb and the misinterpretation of the female name Jedida Elsworth as the masculine "Jedediah" obscured important genealogical clues found in the actual will.[7]

This is not to say that all abstracts have deficiencies similar to the two examples given above, but it is always important to check the original records for errors of omission and interpretation.[8]

---

[6] *Vital Records of New Bedford, Massachusetts to the Year 1850*, 3 vols. (Boston: New England Historical Genealogical Society, 1932), 2:242.

[7] The research that led to this will was conducted on behalf of Peter S. Handy of Addison, Texas and is cited with his permission. Research in census records did show that some of George Handy's children were born in Massachusetts in the 1790s, making the 1791 marriage at New Bedford more attractive.

[8] This example shows that Mrs. Barber, whose contribution to New York genealogy is extensive and well known, was not immune to the occasional error.

Glossary

Although you are probably familiar with the probate process and the basic terminology associated with probate records, some definitions are appropriate to help you determine which records may be helpful. The following terms mirror the probate process. In all cases, more detail can be found in *Black's Law Dictionary* (currently in its ninth edition and published by West Group; see *BlacksLawDictionary.com*).

CTA: Administration with the Will Annexed

If the executor named in a will refused to serve in that position, or died before the probate process ended, an "administration cum testament annexo" (CTA) was necessary. The administrator was charged with overseeing the distribution of the estate according to the decedent's will as if he were named executor.

Dower

Sometimes referred to as the "widow's thirds," dower represented the portion of a man's estate that his wife was entitled to if he died intestate or if she was not satisfied with what she was bequeathed by a husband who died testate. In New York, post-1829 dower records represent the formal application of a widow for her "dower right." They are important records to consult because in order to claim her "dower right" the widow had to demonstrate that the children (if any) of the decedent had received their share—and thus name all the children.

Executor's and Administration Bond

After letters testamentary and of administration were issued, the executor or administrator took out a bond promising to faithfully administer the estate. The bond was a sum of money that the executor or administrator would forfeit if the estate was not faithfully administered. As with all bonds, a surety was required to guarantee the executor's or administrator's performance. The surety was very often a close relative or friend of the executor or administrator.

Guardianship

If a decedent left minor (under age 21) children who stood to inherit property, a guardian for such children was appointed (if the child was under age 14) or chosen by the child (if the child was over age 14). The guardian was very often a close relative.

It is important to note that not every orphaned child required a guardian—just those who had an inheritance to be protected. An orphan with no inherited property was often "bound out" by the overseers of the poor (or other public welfare entity) if not taken in by relatives. The Surrogate's Court usually has no record of such transactions, but such records may exist in other jurisdictions.

Inventory

An important element of business in the administration or probate of an estate was to make an inventory of the property of the decedent. In New York State, inventories were not often recorded; they are found among the loose papers in the probate packet.

Letters Testamentary

When a person died testate (with a will), the executor named in the will applied for "letters testamentary." The issuance of such letters allowed the probate of the estate to proceed. *Note:* After 1830, the "application" started with a petition, described in detail on pages 32–33.

Letters of Administration

When a person died intestate (without a will), the next of kin or other interested party applied for "letters of administration." The issuance of such letters allowed the administration of the estate to proceed. The administrator could be the widow, the eldest son, another relative (including a remarried widow's new husband), or even a creditor. Before 1830, the letters of administration may provide one of the only statements of a relationship. *Note:* After 1830, the "application" started with a petition, described in detail on pages 32–33.

Minutes and Orders

Because the "Probate Packet" is often seen as the "be all and end all" of information for New York probate records, many genealogists often ignore or underutilize the surrogate's court minutes and orders. They are important, however, because they provide the structure for the probate process that produces the documents listed above. They can include record of some or all of the following: the *fact* of applications/petitions for probate/administration or dower; the *fact* of the appointment of an executor or administrator; challenges to the probate of an estate; and the final closing of an estate. There may even be items in the minutes or orders for which the loose papers have been lost.

Probate Packets

For all probate matters recorded in books, original loose papers were filed at the surrogate's court in "probate packets" or "estate files." Loose papers can include wills, bonds, letters, the probate petition (starting in 1830), inventories, accounts, and receipts. These loose papers can provide not only valuable genealogical information, but also a glimpse into the life of the decedent and his or her family. These loose papers do not always survive.

Surrogate's Indexes

Surrogate's Indexes in New York State are almost a record unto themselves. Not only do they provide volume and page numbers for probate matters recorded in books, as well as the estate number for access to probate packets and files, but in the nineteenth century and later they often include the date of death of the decedent. Indexes were often created retroactively, so reference to early estates (pre-1830) may contain less detail.

Index